I0882093

Expressive Form

The mode of utilizing computers in architecture today is vague, inexplicit, and, often, arbitrary. Designers tend to conceptualize entities or processes and then enter, manipulate and print using computer systems. Often, theories of design and form are "translated" into computational ones, merely to participate in the digital fashion. This situation creates confusion, misunderstanding, and inconsistency for both students and practitioners over the appropriate use of computers in architecture and design. Challenging these assumptions, this book offers an appropriate theoretical context for computer-based experimentations, explorations, and form-making. By employing computational and formal theories, the author offers a theoretical bridge between the establishment of the past and the potential of the future.

With the increased use of computers, architecture has found itself in the midst of a plethora of possible uses. This book offers some alternative directions, which combine theoretical inquiry with practical implementation. Notions of exaggeration, hybrid, kinetic, algorithmic, fold and warp are examined from different points of view: historical, mathematical, philosophical or critical.

Expressive Form offers a unique perspective on the use of computers related to aesthetics and specifically to architectural form and design. As an architect, professor and computer scientist, Kostas Terzidis is able to discern the unique and worthwhile features of computation as they apply to the idiosyncratic world of architectural design. He provides a source of inspiration for students and professionals.

Kostas Terzidis is an Assistant Professor in UCLA's Department of Architecture. His work focuses on creative experimentation within the threshold between arts, architecture, and computer science. He has studied extensively the implications of virtual reality for the representation of space and spatiality in art and architecture. He is the author of many computer applications on form-making, morphing, filtering, and network mapping. His most recent work is the development of a visualization system in Java, and a three-dimensional-morphing system. He has presented papers and lectured widely on both virtual reality and algorithmic design systems at conferences, ranging from design methods to engineering applications.

Expressive Form

A conceptual approach to computational design

Kostas Terzidis

Routledge
Taylor & Francis Group
LONDON AND NEW YORK

First published 2003 by Spon Press
This edition published by Routledge 2012
2 Park Square, Milton Park, Abingdon, Oxon OX14 4RN

Simultaneously published in the USA and Canada by Routledge
711 Third Avenue, New York, NY 10017

Routledge is an imprint of the Taylor & Francis Group, an informa business

Typeset in Univers by Florence Production, Stoodleigh, Devon

British Library Cataloguing in Publication Data
A catalogue record for this book is available from the British Library

Library of Congress Cataloging in Publication Data
Terzidis, Kostas, 1962–
Expressive form/Kostas Terzidis
p. cm.
Includes bibliographical references and index.
ISBN 0-415-31743-6 (alk. paper) – ISBN 0-415-31744-4 (pbk: alk. paper)
1. Architecture – Philosophy. 2. Architecture – Mathematics.
3. Architecture – Data processing. 4. Computer-aided design. I. Title.
NA2500.T46 2003
721′.0285 – dc21 2003006155

ISBN 10: 0-415-31743-6 (hb)
ISBN 10: 0-415-31744-4 (pb)

ISBN 13: 978-0-415-31743-6 (hb)
ISBN 13: 978-0-415-31744-3 (pb)

Contents

Foreword

There is an economy of shapes; anyone who has ever worked all night to create design drawings or models on deadline is vividly aware of that. Some shapes are quick and easy to construct with available tools, but others are slow and laborious. Since architects must always produce designs within finite time periods, and with limited expenditure of resources, they are always constrained by the current shape economy.

For many centuries, traditional drafting instruments – straightedge, parallel bar and triangles, scale ruler, protractor, compasses, and dividers – defined the prevailing shape economy. Together with Euclid's geometric construction procedures, these instruments established a manageable shape universe of straight lines and arcs of circles, parallels and perpendiculars, triangles of various kinds, squares, rectangles, regular polygons, and so on. Texts on architectural theory and design technique, from Vitruvius to early modernism, provided introductions to it.

But technological innovations expand and restructure shape economies, as they do other types of economies. When transparent drafting paper became available, it was easier for architects to work with translated, rotated, and reflected instances of shapes; they just moved sheets around, or turned them over, and quickly produced transformed copies by tracing. Gridded paper facilitated creation of modular designs. And the photographic enlarger, followed by the modern photocopier, slashed the time and cost of scale transformations.

In the mid-twentieth century, with the emergence of early computer graphics and computer-aided design systems, a momentous shift from craft to industrial shape economies began. You could think of a typical early CAD system as a shape factory – intended, like other factories, to enhance productivity. It provided the traditional vocabulary of straight lines, circles, and arcs, together with the standard repertoire of Euclidean constructions, and it was faster. Furthermore, it encouraged investment in efficient design machinery; software developers could write procedures that produced standard shapes, then architects could later use those procedures to assemble designs by selecting, transforming, instantiating and combining shapes from the predefined vocabulary. So design offices that installed early CAD technology became less labor intensive and more capital intensive. They could produce designs on shorter schedules and at lower cost, or they could explore more options within the same resource constraints, and they could maintain better quality control, but the shape universe they engaged would have been quite familiar to Vitruvius or Alberti.

Meanwhile, another way to think about the role of computer graphics in design was gaining ground. Curved forms were defined by mathematical functions, so you did not have to restrict yourself to straight lines, arcs, planes, cylinders, spheres, and the like; you could write procedures that efficiently constructed all sorts of exotic curves and surfaces. Furthermore, you could employ CAD/CAM machinery to efficiently produce physical realizations of them. The new shape economy that resulted from this allowed architects to explore a greatly expanded shape universe. At the turn of the century, Frank Gehry's Bilbao Guggenheim Museum provided a spectacular demonstration of the possibilities, and brought them to wide public attention.

More generally, you can write a limitless variety of shape generation procedures that can quickly be executed by computer, but would be impossibly laborious if you tried to execute them by hand. These procedures make use not only of curve-generating functions, but also computational mechanisms such as iteration, recursion, and the conditional application of rules. The more we invest in coding such procedures, the less restrictive the shape economy becomes, and the more extensive and interesting the design domains that architects can explore. This volume introduces shape generation procedures for the architect, classifies them, provides numerous compelling examples, and critically explores their expressive uses. It will be extremely helpful to students and professionals who want to understand the connection between design intentions and computational tools, and who are interested in creating such tools themselves.

And it provokes a crucial question. Who will control the emerging shape economy of the twenty-first century? One possibility is that a few large software developers will dominate the CAD market, treat libraries of shape construction procedures as proprietary intellectual property, and thus define the shape universes that architects can explore. Under this scenario, designers become consumers of standardized, centrally developed and marketed software products, and architectural historians of the future will characterize bodies of architectural work in terms of the software releases that generated them. Alternatively, architects might create shape construction procedures themselves, in decentralized fashion, share them freely within open-source communities, and thus sustain a broad-based, vibrant culture of critical thought and innovation. If you prefer the latter scenario, you should read this book.

William J. Mitchell
Cambridge

Preface

This book is about the notion of expressiveness in architecture through the use of computational and computer-based methods. With the increased use of computers, architecture has found itself in the midst of a plethora of possible uses. The book offers some alternative directions, which combine theoretical inquiry with practical implementation. In this book, some important notions are investigated in the light of their computational and formal value: exaggeration, hybridization, kinesis, algorithm, fold, and warp. Each notion is examined from different points of view – historical, mathematical, or philosophical. The pedagogical value of this book is to serve as a source of inspiration for students and professionals.

The book offers a unique perspective on the use of computers related to architectural form and design. My background as an architect, a professor, and a computer scientist allows me to discern the unique and worthwhile features of computation as they apply to the idiosyncratic world of architectural design.

The mode of utilizing computers in architecture today is vague, inexplicit, and, often, arbitrary. Entities or processes that are already conceptualized in the designer's mind are entered, manipulated, and printed using computer systems. Often, theories of design and form are "translated" into computational ones, merely to participate in the digital fashion. This situation creates confusion, misunderstanding, and inconsistency for both students and practitioners over the appropriate use of computers in architecture and design. Challenging these assumptions, the book offers an appropriate theoretical context for computer-based experimentations, explorations, and form-making. By employing computational and formal theories, such as those of kinetic, algorithmic, hybrid, folded or warped form, the author offers a theoretical bridge between the establishment of the past and the potential of the future.

Kostas Terzidis

Los Angeles

Introduction

Expressive is a term that differs from, but is often confused with, dynamic.[1] While dynamism implies animation, motion, and action, expressiveness embodies some of the most intrinsic, existential, and unique qualities of form: *character* and *identity*. Expressiveness is about personality, individuality, and idiosyncrasy. In its connotative implications, it captures the ontological spirit of form and its shaping forces. It manifests form's meaning, significance, and quintessence.

Unlike dynamism, which illustrates change, activity, or progress, expressiveness implies tendency, inclination, propensity, disposition, or proclivity. Rather than being related to an actual event, expressiveness signifies a special moment in time when an event is about to happen. It is about the notions of likelihood, probability, expectation, anticipation, eagerness, or suspense. In a deeper sense expressiveness is about transcendence, extraordinariness, reminiscence, resemblance, and traceability.

The power of expressiveness lies primarily in its connotative and subliminal value. Expressiveness is closely associated with the notions of implicit, inferred, suggestive, unsaid, tacit, and unspoken. In its largest sense, it signifies not only the articulated, the unambiguous, the directly and distinctly stated, but also that which cannot be shown or said through spoken words, or that which does not need words to convey its meaning. By extension it signifies that whose appearance or behavior is rooted in means that cannot be verbalized, or lie beyond, or are redundant, or are unknown, or follow from principles outside previous understanding. Expressiveness is not only about what is seen but also about what is not seen, not only about what is understood but also about what is not (yet) understood. Etymologically, the root of the word "express-" can be traced to the prefix "ex-", which means "not from" or "outside", and the word "press" which points indirectly to the notion of "phrase".[2] In that sense, expressiveness demarcates the end of the spoken and the beginning of the unspoken or vice versa. Any form of expression or any expression of form pushes the boundaries of previous understanding by building up new verbal or formal articulations.

Tacit is a term that differs from, but is often confused with, the term *implicit.* While "implicit" suggests the presence of absence, "tacit" involves the shaping forces of connotative understanding. Tacit arises by operations of cultural values rather than through indirect expression. In many forms of expression, tacit messages are transmitted in lieu of literal messages. Ordinary expressions may employ verbal interaction, but tacit expression often utilizes awkward behavior, such as meaningful silence, body language, or cultural assumptions as means of transmitting information.[3] For instance, designers often use non-verbal means of expression such as sketches, drawings, analogies, gestures, or metaphors. What makes verbal expression so problematic for creative people is that it is too literal, leaving little, if any, ground for interpretation. It assumes that for every notion or idea there is a word or a phrase to describe it, but that may not be the case for *yet to be defined* creative concepts. In contrast, both implicit and tacit expressions suggest much more than their spoken counterparts.

Similarly, form is not always conceived literally as made out of matter. In fact, form is rather an abstract entity that possesses certain geometric characteristics. The attachment of material qualities constrains the behavior of form and restricts the designer's imagination. In contrast, the lack of materiality liberates form from its constraints and introduces behaviors closer to intuition rather than perception. Furthermore, skillful omission or deliberate inclusion of partial information creates patterns of interpretation that engage the viewer to participate in the visual composition by "connecting the dots". Even though form may be often conceived as an autonomous geometric entity, use of alternative terms, such as "formation", "configuration", "pattern", or "arrangement" allow a broader understanding of the tacit nature of form.

Recent theories of form in architecture have focused on computational methods of formal exploration and expression. From "topological geometry" and hypersurfaces to blobs and folds, there is a clear tendency to seek and explore formal properties as sources of ordering systems. For the last two decades, beginning with Marcos Novak's "Computational Compositions" (1988), William Mitchell's *Logic of Architecture* (1990), and Peter Eisenman's "Visions Unfolding" (1992), and continuing through John Frazer's *An Evolutionary Architecture* (1995) and Greg Lynn's *Animate Form* (1999) to name a few, designers have been concerned with the use of computational mechanisms for the exploration of formal systems.[4] These practices have attempted to readdress formal issues using new techniques and methods.

Computational tools are central protagonists in this exploration. The traditional problematic of space, form, and order is informed, reformed, and transformed by the new possibilities and strategies open through technological cross-pollination, particularly digital technologies and a new computational relationship to space and time.[5] The theoretical possibilities cut across disciplines and are affected by concepts and mechanisms that have no precedence. In response to architecture's striving to critically embrace and understand the new formal possibilities, two approaches have been dominant: either a reevaluation of past theories and practices in search of parallel or reoccurring themes, or a search for new unprecedented themes that derive their existence from concepts and mechanisms foreign, alien, or external to the discipline of architecture.

The first approach builds upon historical precedence and seeks to metaphorically or indirectly associate past concepts in a new context, ultimately aiming at establishing historical continuity, transformation, and evolution. It approaches digital tools as recording and representational devices at the service of human creativity and interpretation. Human dominance over the machine is a necessary assumption in order to explain phenomena and construct interpretations. Within the human realm, any logic that deals with the evaluation or production of form must be, by default, both understandable and open to interpretation. The problem with this approach is that it does not allow thoughts to transcend beyond the sphere of human understanding. In fact, while it praises and celebrates the uniqueness and complexity of the human mind, it also becomes resistant to theories that point out the potential limitations of the human mind. For instance, in *Warped Spaces,* Vidler looks at current architectural formal experimentations in the light of digital techniques but relies heavily on psychoanalytical thought and artistic interpretation.[6] By doing so the author engages himself to investigate the complexity of the human mind but fails to extend beyond that and engage into inquiring about the ontological aspects of the "digital mind" and the increasing dependency on its alien nature by designers and architects.

In contrast, the second approach builds towards a new theoretical framework necessary to evaluate computational mechanisms critically by seeking evidence beyond previous understanding and outside the context of predictable events. Digital devices are seen not as tools for exploring what is *known* but as portals for entering into what is *unknown*. Computational mechanisms are employed not only for exploring formal concepts but also for forming new concepts. For instance, the discovery of the "hypercube" resulted from an inductive process of projection that mapped three-dimensional points of a cube into four-dimensional ones. And yet, indeed, both the projections and the resulting hypercube are neither predictable nor observable. In this sense, computational devices become portals for exploration of forms that extends beyond the limits of perception. What makes this approach problematic for architects is that they have maintained an ethos of artistic sensibility and intuitive playfulness in their practice. Because of its mechanistic nature, computational mechanisms are perceived as non-human creations and therefore are considered distant and remote.

Lying between and yet harmonizing these dialectically opposed strategies is the notion of expressiveness that involves both digital experimentation and human interpretation. In searching for and appreciating the notion of expressiveness one cannot ignore the complexity of the human mind and yet cannot neglect the potential of the digital creator. Expressive form is the result of a synergy between the creator and the viewer, for without one another "expressive" or "form" cannot exist.

The aim of this book is to explore the duality of expressive forms. It sets out to reintroduce old concepts in the light of new insights. Caricature, kinetic, hybrid, folded, and algorithmic are notions that provide rich background to be investigated in the light of computational mechanisms. Thus skillful exaggeration, virtual motion, meaningful hybridization, masterly folding, and algorithmic induction, using the appropriate visual depiction, will be investigated for their artistic, architectural, and computational value.

First, the notion of a caricature and its expressive value will be discussed. Caricature is an exaggeration, a skillfully stretched and intentionally deformed alteration of a familiar form. In our present technological age, there are computer tools that allow one to *deform*, *disturb*, and *alter* shapes in almost any perceivable way. A question arises as to whether there are some special deformations that we as humans interpret as dramatic and expressive. Traditionally, caricature provides a medium of expression that is subtle, implicit, connotative, and indirect, yet powerful, expressive, and emotive. Since caricature design employs formal logic in its conception and interpretation, a leap into the alien world of computational possibilities may exhort, stir, and inspire personality and character in inanimate objects that are not, by nature, *interesting*.

Next, the process of morphing will be explored. *Morphing* is a term used to describe a process in which an object changes its form gradually in order to obtain another form. It is a gradual transition that results in a marked change in the form's appearance, character, condition, or function. Morphing is a powerful formal device that embodies one of architecture's most existential struggles: to express and identify itself through its own form. The result of morphing is a hybrid object, which combines characteristics of both parent objects involved in the transformation. Computationally, morphing can be described as a bi-univocal and bi-continuous correspondence between the points of the respective figures maintaining the connection and vicinity of the points of the figure. The essence of such a transformation lies not in the parents' forms but rather in the intermediate phases these transformations pass through, as well as in the extrapolations, which go beyond the parents' forms. It is the transitional continuity of a form that expresses it own history and existence through a series of evolutionary stages.

Following this the notion of kinetic form will be investigated. Kinetic is a term used to describe a situation related to, or produced by, motion. Kinetic form is not a contradiction but rather an extension to the notion of form as a motionless boundary. It is about the idea that perpetual succession is not only conceived directly through physical motion but also indirectly through formal expression. Juxtaposition, superimposition, sequence, friction, deformation, resistance, absence, aftereffect, and progression are some of the visual manifestations of kinetic expression. The study of kinetic form may benefit from the use of computational tools. Simulated dynamic environments, particle behavior, fields, finite elements, complex deformations, rendering techniques, and mathematical surfaces are some of the many processes and mechanisms available today for exploration and experimentation.

Next, the notions of folding, unfolding, and bending will be analyzed. *Folding* is an intricate process that addresses one of form's most existential qualities: the cross from one dimension into another, for example a two-dimensional sheet of paper folded into a three-dimensional composition. In contrast, *unfolding* is a term used to denote the process of opening, spreading out, or extending something folded. Rather than approaching folding or unfolding as isolated operations, they should be understood as a complementary unified pair, the importance of which lies "in between" as the one operation owes its existence to the absence (or the potential existence) of the other. Furthermore, the possibility of using kinematics opens up a more intricate relationship between (un)folding and motion. While the dominant mode for discussing the notion of folding in architecture has been that of an aesthetics paradigm, the use of kinematics, implemented through folding schemes, may challenge the very nature of what architecture really is.

Visual depiction as means of expression will then be discussed. Artists and designers engage in storytelling and offer a glimpse into their fantasy worlds through unique, personal, private, and idiosyncratic visual methods. The computer has already proven to be useful as both a representational and a visualization tool to designers, but the introduction of computational methods to represent three-dimensional forms is not simply a visual phenomenon. The visual qualities of computer-generated forms may be impressive, exotic, or magical, but it seems misguided to confuse their internal representation with their visual appearance. While phenomena may be indicative of certain behaviors, appearances are, usually, deceiving.

Finally, algorithmic logic will be examined as a mode of thought. An algorithm is a computational procedure for addressing a problem in a finite number of steps. It involves deduction, induction, abstraction, generalization, and structured logic. It is the systematic extraction of logical principles and the development of a generic solution plan. While most algorithms are tailored to automate tedious manual methods, there is a certain category of algorithms that are not aimed at predictable results. Their inductive strategy is to explore generative processes or to simulate complex phenomena. Such inductive algorithms can be regarded as extensions to human thinking and therefore may allow one to leap into areas of unpredictable, unimaginable, and, often, inconceivable potential. Similarly in design, mathematical models, topological properties, genetic systems, mappings, and morphisms are algorithmic processes aimed at exploring uncommon, unpredictable, and uncharted formal properties and behaviors.

Computational formal explorations do not eradicate human imagination but rather extend its potential limitations. Computation is not a substitute for human creativity and therefore cannot be antagonistic. Rather it provides the means for

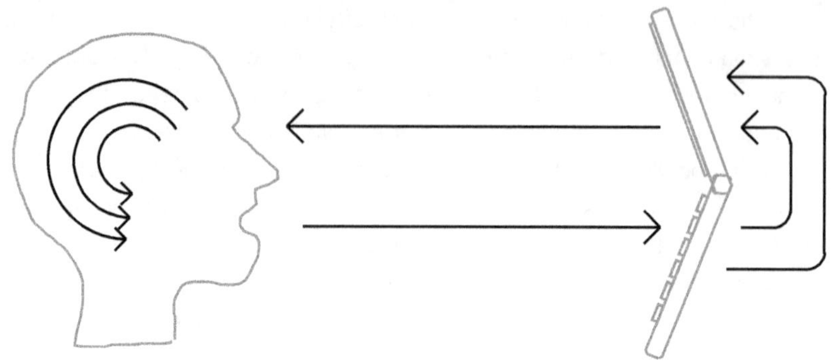

exploration, experimentation, and investigation in an alternative realm. For the first time perhaps, form might be aligned with neither arbitrary creativity nor computational determinism but with creative computation and computational creativity.

I.1
Computational formal explorations do not eradicate human imagination but rather extend its potential limitations

Conversely, human intuition is characterized by originality, expressiveness, and imagination. While in the human world intuition has been an underlying assumption for many design activities, in the world of computation a more rational, confined, organized, and methodical model exists. It suggests efficiency, effectiveness, and productivity, while, at the same time, it may be resistant to emotion, humor, irony, metaphor, or analogy.

As the world of design is starting to shift from the "manual" model toward the "computerized" model, a need arises to integrate two seemingly contrasting worlds, that of intuition and that of computation. What makes computation so problematic for design theorists is that it has maintained an ethos of *rationalistic determinism* – the theory that the exercise of reason provides the only valid basis for action or belief and that reason is the prime source of knowledge – in its field. Because of its clarity and efficiency, rationalistic determinism has traditionally been a dominant mode of thought in the world of computation. The problem with this approach is that it assumes that all computational activities abide by the same principles. In contrast, intuition, as defined in the arts and design, is based on quite different, if not opposing, principles. Rather than following a rationalistic model, designers often employ the acceptance of empiricism, authority, spiritual revelation, metaphor or analogy as sources for their inspiration. In addition, they quite often defy the rules of precision, planning, and scheduling. This mode of thought comes in contrast to the dominant computational model where methodical, predictable, and dividable processes exist. More than ever now, as design intuition enters the computational world, a complementing and harmonious mix of both thought processes is needed.

Notes

1 Arnheim suggests expression through dynamics. See Arnheim, R., *The Dynamics of Architectural Form*, Berkeley: University of California Press, 1977, p. 253.

2 In Greek, the word "expression" is "*ek-phrasis*", that is, a combination of the prefix "*ek-*" or *ex-* and the root "*phrasis*" or phrase.

3 A powerful example is a scene from David Lynch's *Mulholland Drive* (2001). In that movie, Naomi Watts performs a piece for an audition in two very different ways. Using the exact same script she expresses two totally antithetical emotions: anger and hate versus passion and lust.

4 See Novak, M., "Computational Compositions", in *Computing in Design Education, ACADIA '88 Workshop Proceedings*, ed. P.J. Bancroft, Ann Arbor, University of Michigan, October 1988, pp. 5–30; Mitchell, W., *Logic of Architecture*, Cambridge, MA: MIT Press, 1990 and Eisenmann, P., "Visions' Unfolding: Architecture In The Age Of Electronic Media", *Domus*, vol. 734, 1992, pp. 17–24. Also see Frazer, J., *An Evolutionary Architecture*, London: Architectural Association, 1995; and Lynn, G., *Animate Form*, New York: Princeton Architectural Press, 1999.

5 An interesting article that points out the new computational relationship to space and time is Lonsway's "Mistaken Dimensionality". In it, Lonsway detects incompleteness in the digital representation of space and time using commercial applications, and inquires into extending the literal coordinate dimensions into a realm where an "n-dimensional framework" captures the essence of computational space. See Lonsway, B., "The Mistaken Dimensionality of CAD", *Journal of Architectural Education*, vol. 56, issue 2, November 2002, pp. 22–25.

6 See Vidler, A., *Warped Spaces*, Cambridge, MA: MIT Press, 1999.

Chapter 1

Caricature Form

Caricature is a term used to describe an exaggeration, a skillfully stretched and intentionally deformed alteration of a familiar form. While caricature is associated with the resulting sketch and its contextual meaning, the art of caricature involves the forces of deformation and their connotative value. In its generative stage, caricature touches one of architectural design's deepest desires: to build life into lifeless forms. In its manifold implications, caricature touches many of architecture's most deeply embedded assumptions about its existence: the struggle of architectural form to stand out, inspire, and identify itself. Traditionally the struggle of architecture has been to express its form through its function without disturbing the balance between the two. Forms convey strong visual messages that are intrinsically associated with their formal characteristics. What makes a caricature so polemic for architects is that the modern movement has imposed a strong concern towards the dominance of form. The importance of form in architecture, as opposed to function and content, has the advantage of taking into account the idiosyncratic links of architecture to its major relative, art. The disadvantage, however, is that formalism, among Modern theorists, has connotations of being too iconolatric, superficial, and conformist. As a consequence, formalism has always been regarded suspiciously as combining the icons of historical architecture and technological development at a surface level.

Challenging these concerns, a caricature is a celebration of form at its most existential level. It provides a medium of expression that is subtle, implicit, connotative, and indirect, yet powerful, expressive, and emotional. Because of its highly connotative nature, caricature's power lies in the value of its subliminal messages. A successfully exaggerated figure provides the means of expression that can stir emotions and attract attention. It is analogous to poetry. A caricature deformation is not simply an alteration of an existing form but rather an implicit juxtaposition of a familiar archetype. The notion of familiarity plays an important role, as it becomes the basis of comparison between the original and the deformed. As in poetry, the power of caricature lies not only in the presence of formal features but also in the subtle presence of their absence.

Caricature differs from, but is often confused with, cartoon. While cartoon implies context and action, caricature involves the exaggeration of a form and its shaping forces; it suggests personality, character, identity, distinctiveness, individuality, and connotation. In cartoon, it is the sequence of events that lead, to a result, whereas in caricature it is the figure itself that implies an emotion. In architecture, the discussion on cartoons follows the strip or cinematic model, where the multiplication and sequencing of static frames lead to a humorous situation. The problem with this model is that architecture occupies the role of the static frame through which motion progresses. In contrast, caricature *is* the static frame through which motion is implied.

In many fields of design, "caricaturization" is a common practice. In industrial, automotive, manufacture, and graphics design, to name but a few, the end product is intentionally exaggerated to suggest indirectly a certain visual effect. In automotive design, for example, the space of design is conceived as a deformable grid that can mimic the shape, posture, or pose of animals or human silhouettes.[1] While physical form is defined in terms of mathematical surfaces, the virtual archetype of the environment in which it is designed contributes to its shape. The static Cartesian system of architecture is replaced by the dynamic design space of engineering. Forms are conceived in their totality and not as collections of constituent components.

Likewise, the forms of a dynamically conceived architecture may be shaped through deformations of virtual archetypes. Actual sculpture involves chiseling marble, modeling clay, or casting in metal, whereas virtual sculpture allows form to occupy a multiplicity of possible formations continuously within the same form. This concept of a soft form, which can be selectively deformed in design space, is radically different from the idea of a rigid archetype. The soft form is a result of an infinite continuum of possible variations. The assignment of particular variables governs its internal structure. The form in flux is possible by defining its geometry parametrically. Once conscious of the immaterial constitution of the object, once conscious of its not being marble, clay, metal or glass, but only a three-dimensional representation of reality, a topological morphology is conceivable and possible.

The term deformation is often used in a negative sense. It implies the degradation or perversion of a "healthy" figure. In architecture, deformation is a term often used to denounce a fundamental change in the structure of a form. The prefix "de-" often implies departure from a common practice and suggests challenging an established status quo. In that context, the term deformation is not a negation, but rather an affirmation. It implies an *alternative* way of creating form.

In virtual design space, deformation is conceived as a proportional redistribution of points along a direction. The notions of "redistribution" and "direction" imply the existence of time as a measure of comparison. In order to conceive the change dictated by the deformation it is important still to recognize the previous state of the form, before the deformation occurred. The true value of a deformation is not in the end result but in the infinitesimal slice of time where past and present overlap within the same form.

In all of these threshold conditions of time, a superimposition of the viewer's interpretation is put into relation such that the deformed shapes are conceived through the impression of real motion. Although form is conceived of as static when observed as discrete pictures, the viewer's experience of form is interactive and dynamic. Deformation suggests the superimposition of invisible forces in the same way that soft clay implies the hands of a sculptor. The attributes of softness, elasticity, plasticity and flexibility imply the act of deformation.

Historically, exaggerations of the human figure, or parts of it, were used to convey political or religious messages, such as power, divinity, terror, fertility, sexuality, and so on. By implying a quantitative interpretation of form, any exaggeration in size, shape, or attribute automatically suggests a corresponding exaggeration of the signified form's quality: the bigger something looks, the more important it is, and vice versa. Thus, the demarcation of extremes establishes a ground for comparisons.

The model of quantitative exaggeration is based on the profound linear relationship between size and importance. It is also possible that exaggerations may occur in the form of proportional alterations. One of the first "caricaturists" to study the effects of proportion on the human face was Albrecht Dürer. What is remarkable about his studies is that he used a dynamic grid to investigate the relationship between face and geometry. Instead of enumerating faces as isolated events and then trying to connect them, he used geometry as the medium of investigation. By altering the proportions of the grid, Dürer was able to create various caricature faces of existing or non-existing persons.

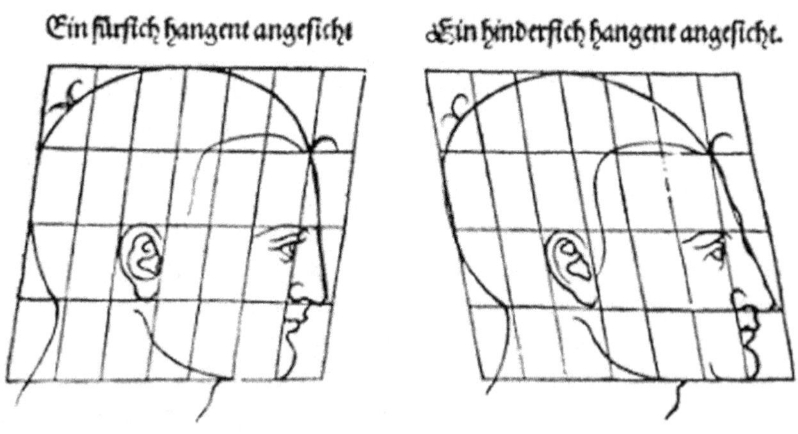

1.1
Alterations of the proportions of geometry affect the human figure, features, and facial expression
(From Albrecht Dürer's treatise on proportion, *Les Quatres livres d'Albrecht Dürer de la proportion des parties et pourtraicts des corps humains*, Arnheim, 1613)

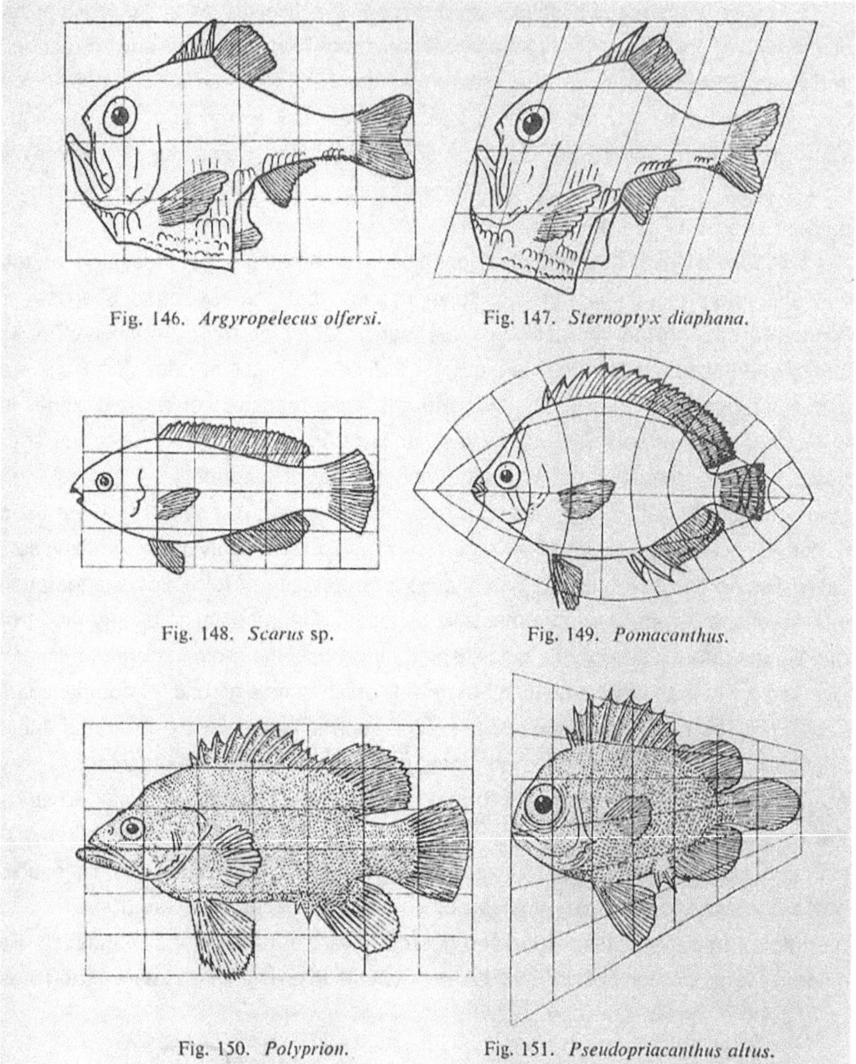

Fig. 146. *Argyropelecus olfersi.* Fig. 147. *Sternoptyx diaphana.* Fig. 148. *Scarus* sp. Fig. 149. *Pomacanthus.* Fig. 150. *Polyprion.* Fig. 151. *Pseudopriacanthus altus.*

1.2
Geometrical manipulations of species' evolution instances

In the work of biologists we see similar studies of deformations, alteration, and *unintended* caricatures of animals and organisms. Even though the biologists' intention was to find missing links or continuity in species, from a formal point of view the grids and guides used to describe the process of evolution offer a glimpse into a world of caricature. What is interesting about these studies is the use of non-linear systems of deformation based on proportional alterations of a superimposed mesh. Curvature becomes more important than linear scaling. Under these systems, even inanimate objects, such as bones or fossils, can be seen as caricatures.[2]

Even though humans and animals appear relatively easy candidates to *caricaturize,* given their strong expressive nature, a challenge arises for inanimate objects. How can a lifeless form appear to have lifelike properties? The cartoon industry has a rich history of inanimate caricature characters. From candles that dance to cookies that hide, inanimate objects seem to be able to possess human characteristics. The strategy often is simple: attachment of a face or use of a human posture to give character. Similarly, in Disneyland's Toontown, buildings are caricaturized by applying deformations similar to the ones used to create favorite characters: Mickey's home, for example, has strong curves, clumsy postures, and thick frames.

In the work of architect Antonio Gaudi, inanimate forms such as chimneys, roofs, windows, or balconies are deformed to imply an organic caricature effect. Similarly, in the work of architect Frank Gehry, curves and manifolds imply posture and personality. The body language of the towers in Prague nicknamed Fred and Ginger implies the intermingled postures of dancers Fred Astaire and Ginger Rogers. Resting lightly on top of slender columns, the glass tower, with its pinched waist, leans gracefully towards a proud cylindrical tower.

Irony is a term used to indicate the use of a pattern to express something different from, and often opposite to, its literal meaning. It is a special juxtaposition of form and content where one expresses the opposite of the other. The power of irony, as a subliminal mechanism, is based in its contrasting yet comparative nature. In the art of caricature, irony is often used as a means of formal expression. Within all possible alterations of form, some stand out as representations of irony. Surprisingly, representation itself is a form of depiction that represents something else. In the special case that it represents the opposite of what one would expect, it becomes ironic.[3]

In architecture, the use of an established archetype with a symbolic content can function as a source for irony through caricature deformations. Ideally, for modern theorists, the form of a building represents its content. Throughout the history of architecture, certain forms have been associated with certain types of buildings. The deformation of a symbol or its meaning has a dramatic ironic effect. A factory, for example, has a certain organization, structure, shape, and texture that identifies its existence. Most importantly it is a symbol of the working class and as such it carries a strong connotative value. Any deformation of the form of a symbol carries strong connotative repercussions. It is that relationship, between form and content, that allows formal ironic statements to be made. In the work of the Italian architect Aldo Rossi, primitive forms with strong symbolic architectural meaning, such as chimneys, pyramid roofs, colonnades, and flags, are being used by the architect to construct buildings whose function is often the opposite of what they symbolize.[4] A school with a chimney or a federal building that looks like a factory is an ironic architectural statement. In that context, the primitive Euclidean forms play the role of the formal identifier, while its function plays the role of the social identifier.

Caricature design employs formal logic in its conception and interpretation. It is based on formal relationships filtered through layers of interpretation.

1.3
"Toontown" in Disneyland, California

Specifically, deformation and exaggeration are compositional operations that affect the relationships among key elements of the caricature. The operations define the composition and the composition implies the operations. That is why regardless of race, size, or gender, any person deformed in a certain way will look cute. In reverse, cuteness is associated with certain proportions that are, in turn, the result of certain deformation operations.

In Euclidean geometry, form is conceived as the result of a system of abstract relationships. Forms represent idealized versions of conceptual patterns and not perceivable objects. The formal relationships that define primitive shapes are based on the condition of *stasis*, or balance of conceptual forces. Euclidean primitives describe special conditions where an equilibrium state has been obtained. A sphere is not about roundness but rather about the equal distance of points from a central point. The ellipse, which in Greek means *omission*, reflects a "failure" to obtain the equilateral equilibrium of a sphere.

In the world of caricature, Euclidean forms play the role of a point of reference to an archetype. The condition of equilibrium reflects certain formal quali-

1.4
Towers in Prague, nicknamed Fred and Ginger, imply the intermingled postures of dancers Fred Astaire and Ginger Rogers

ties that are associated with the states of initialization or termination. Stability, discreteness, and timelessness are qualities of primitive shapes, which, in turn, are associated with security, steadiness, and durability. These qualities are the basis of reference for formal deformations, as they become the measure of departure from the original state or the proximity of arrival toward the final state. Considering a verbal description, for example, of Gehry's Fred and Ginger building, it may involve a phrase such as "a cylinder with a pinched waist that leans gracefully toward another proud cylindrical tower". Geometrically, the corresponding formal event involves "a thin cylinder bulged inward around its center, then sheared backward and toward another thick cylinder tapered at its base and bulged at the top".

A direct way of defining new forms in Euclidean geometry is through linear or curvilinear transformations of primitives. Equal scaling, for example, of all three-dimensional components, creates similar forms that differ in size. Size, as we pointed out earlier, is associated with quantity. Caricature design uses the measure of size, either relative or absolute, as a means of exaggeration. Differential scaling, on the other hand, allows a selective exaggeration of size. The variation of the proportions of a form can produce a variety of interpretations. Slim, slender shapes suggest grace and elegance, whereas womb-like round shapes suggest warmth or comfort. A form tilted forward may suggest aggression or curiosity, whereas the same shape tilted backward may suggest fear or concern. The interrelationship between primitive forms and primitive emotions is of great importance in caricature design. It involves a dialectic definition of emotion which assumes that certain forms are alive, while our experience of them may be the opposite. Alive becomes the condition of form acted on by emotion, while lifeless becomes the condition of form resting in equilibrium. Both positions assume that emotion is something which can be added or subtracted from form.

Euclidean transformations, such as movement, rotation, scaling, or reflection, incubate within a closed, isolated and hermetic environment, while forms, under the influence of transformations, may change in shape, size, direction, or orientation – no parts are added or subtracted from the scene. It is the forces of deformation that change, not the integrity of the objects. In contrast, Boolean operations are constructive or deconstructive tools that allow new elements to be added to a scene and others to be removed. Addition suggests superimposition, whereas subtraction implies the presence of absence. For caricature design, Boolean operations allow the notions of absence or presence to be implied, which, in turn, allow time to be imprinted on form. "Before" and "after" are simply the results of a set operation where the parent's ghosts are still present in the shapes of its children. A mold, for example, is the negative of a positive form, neither of which would exist without the other. Set operations are not part of the Euclidean world *per se*. Contrary to the idealized immaterial existence of forms in Euclidean geometry, Boolean operations incorporate the behavior of matter. In that sense, their apprehension is connected to our empirical experience of matter and its properties. In the work of architect Richard Meyer, for example, we often see disturbances of the four- or nine-square "equilibrium" scheme. By shifting or subtracting a square from the initial static scheme, a series of dynamic consequences occur that try to bring the scheme back to a state of equilibrium. This reaction involves a material response to a dynamic change in the design environment.

Another way that a caricature form can express its dynamism is through its external skin. Deformation, fluctuation, ripples and chills can be constructed by simulating the behavior of membranes or thin plates. Finite elements on the surface

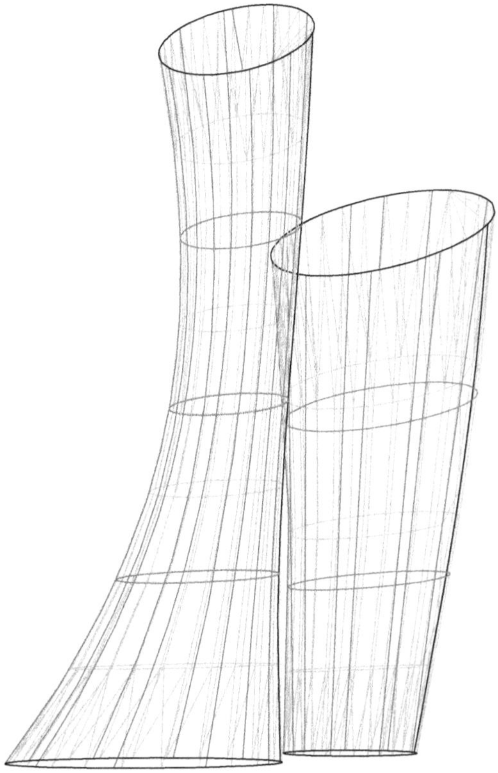

1.5
A thin cylinder bulged inward around its center, then sheared backward and toward another thick cylinder tapered at its base and bulged at the top

of a skin, called *patches*, are associated with springs of individually controllable stiffness. The resulting surface is a network of springs that stretches, bends, loops, twists, and eventually loosens and adapts to external forces. Softness, roughness, stiffness and gentleness are characteristics of caricature forms. Plasticity, elasticity, and flexibility are dynamic parameters controlled through the sequential continuity of variables.

The sequential continuity of a series of variables interacting with one another poses a problem that only some sort of a "fluid" geometry can answer. The work of Gauss, Riemann, von Helmholtz, and Clifford showed that geometries could be based on relationships other than Euclidean. Differential geometry is the study of geometrical forms using the methods of calculus. This alters the notion of geometry by revealing its abstract postulational character and removes it from any connection with the structure of empirical intuition. Forms can be constructed on the basis of non-Euclidean axioms, revealing behaviors closer to our sensations than our perception. For example, if we assume that visual space is hyperbolic and physical space is Euclidean, it is possible to derive a comparative model of mapping between the two spaces, allowing a totally different conceptualization of form. Such a model is expressed as a hyperbolic transformation applied to Euclidean/Cartesian shapes of the physical environment. The result is a hallucinating view of pictorial space where every form in the scene *appears* to be a caricature.[5]

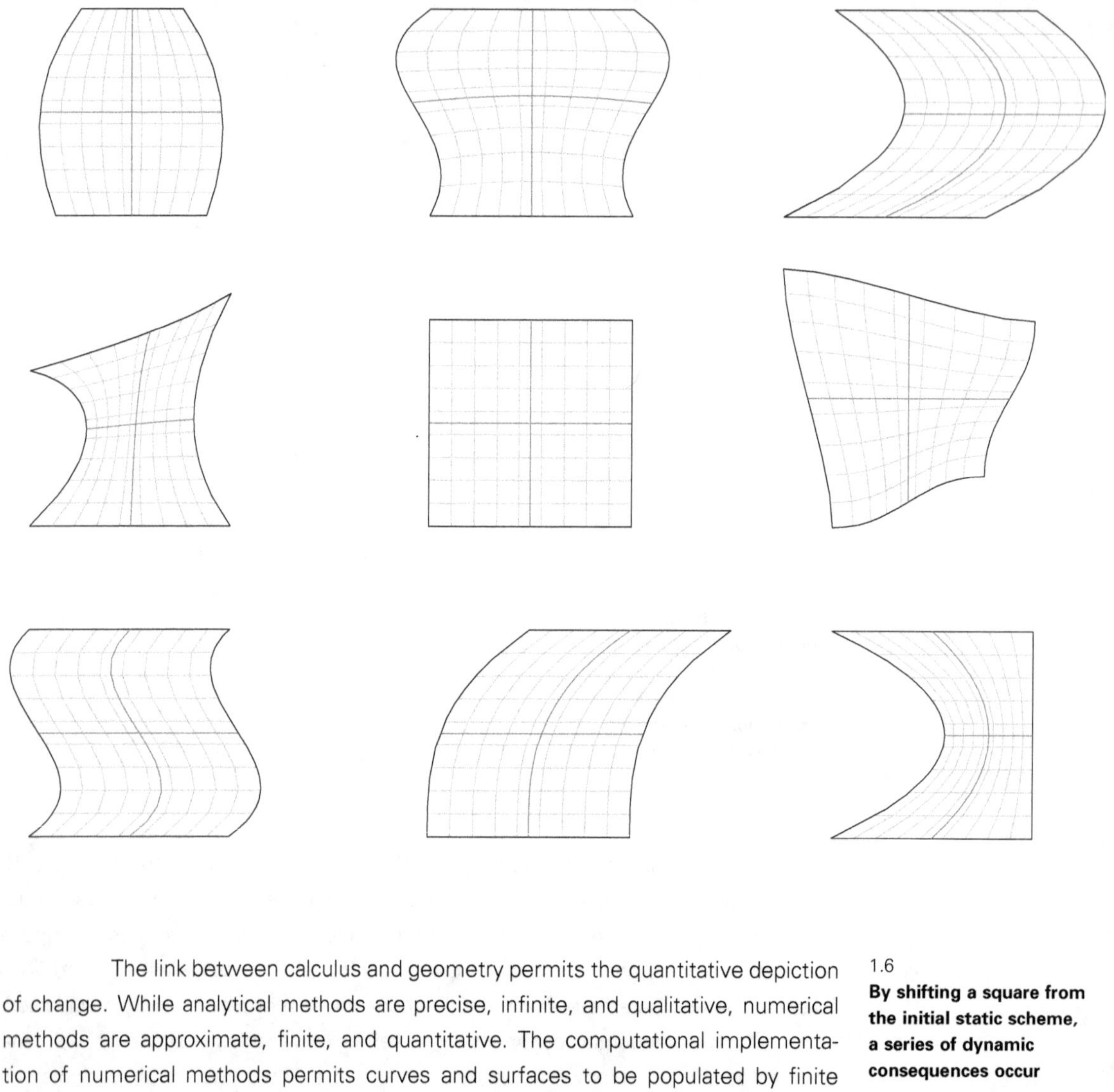

1.6
By shifting a square from the initial static scheme, a series of dynamic consequences occur

The link between calculus and geometry permits the quantitative depiction of change. While analytical methods are precise, infinite, and qualitative, numerical methods are approximate, finite, and quantitative. The computational implementation of numerical methods permits curves and surfaces to be populated by finite elements that approximate their curvature. The blending functions represent their sequential continuity and the control points their physical location. It is from that dialectic relationship between the ideal and the real that caricature form derives its implicit nature. As the physical location of a control point is transformed, the blending functions retain the continuity of the surface, hence preserving the topological identity of the deformed object.[6]

While topology is the study of those properties of geometrical objects that remain unchanged under continuous transformations of the object, the notion of topological forms as soft and plastic is slightly incorrect. The plastic forms, often depicted in books on topology, reflect simply implementations of topological operations between or within forms. Nonetheless, the elastic properties of these theoretical forms are closely related to caricature form. Homogeneity, for example,

1.7
Fish-eye view of a building

is a property that allows a shape to be deformed quite extensively and yet to retain its topological identity. This property asserts an archetypal identity that retains continuity in perception throughout the transformations. As we have pointed out earlier, caricature form is tightly connected to its interpretation. Topology allows the abstract definition of form through its own properties. As long as these properties are retained the form is identifiable.

The use of *implicit surfaces* and *weights* is a relatively new method to represent parametric surfaces with topological properties using implicit forces. A *meta-ball*, for example, is a parametric surface with a scalar field. Its behavior can be described as plastic, flexible, and soft. Depending on its weight, it can attract or repel its neighbors. A meta-ball form is the result of the convolution of two continuous parametric surfaces positive on the inside and negative on the outside. Their "blobby" properties and their ability to be combined in Boolean-like operations are ideal for caricature design. In the work of Bernhard Franken and the Kolatan MacDonald Studio we see attempts to express architecture through soft, smooth, force-bounded shapes. The stiffness, discreteness, and orthogonality of modern architecture are replaced by the smooth, continuous, and round.

The creation of architecture can soon cease to be seen as the creation of isolated spatial events. The creation of systems of relationships and the assignment of specific values will become the foreground of the architect's activity and invention. The new soft and workable object negates the singularity of the old rigid object and asserts the freedom of an open system where change is celebrated.[7] New emphasis is placed on curvature and proportion and therefore on organic and dynamic relations. The surprise of the unexpected result infuses new energy to the act of designing as well as experiencing architecture.

More than ever now, through the use of computer tools and manufacturing techniques, architecture finds itself in a position to rediscover and challenge its traditional values. Architects are presented with tools that allow them to manipulate the overall order and organization of their buildings, thus replacing a single design with a range of designs. The creation of a building does not follow from the placement of individual elements but from the ordering of formal systems. In our present age, there are computer tools that allow us to *deform*, *disturb*, and *alter* shapes in almost any perceivable way. A question arises as to whether there are some special deformations that we as humans interpret as dramatic and expressive. If that is true, then we may be able to create an architecture of caricature.

Traditionally in mainstream architecture, static, expressive-less forms dominate our cities. The common practice for architects is to deliver a functionally sound building with little if any attention paid to the formal aspects of the building. Unfortunately, most buildings are passive boxes with no spirit or persona. They do not "talk". They have nothing to say about themselves; about what they are, where they are coming from, or what they want to be. Perhaps through the use of computational design tools we can inspire personality and character in inanimate objects that are not, by their nature, *interesting*.

Notes

1 Motorcycle design has a rich tradition in exaggerating features of animals, birds, reptiles, or insects. You can look into the following models: Cobra Trakker, Suzuki Hayabusa, Morbidelli V-8, Honda Super Cub, and the Britten V1000.

2 See Thompson, D., *On Growth and Form*, Cambridge: Cambridge University Press, 1961, p. 299.

3 In the last chapter of Bertrand Russell's *Introduction to Mathematical Logic*, New York: Dover Publications, 1920, p. 194, there is a section on formal logic. Formal logic is a branch of logic concerned with problems of syllogismic validity, that is, whether sequences of thoughts lead to valid conclusions. Russell argues that *the validity of a syllogism is independent of the truth or falsity of the premises*. This is expressed by representing the *form* of a syllogism, independent of its *content*. We can say that the "form" of a proposition is that which remains unchanged when every constituent of the proposition is replaced by another. In Ionescu's theatre of the absurd all arbitrary acts are guided through an unorthodox logic, a kind of deformed reasoning. A man and a woman, for example, are sitting next to each other chatting. It is only after a terrible sequence of coincidences that they realize they are husband and wife. Similarly, in the work of the Dadaist Kurt Schwitters, we find strong suggestions of compositional formal logic. He collects a number of garbage tins, clothes and old newspapers. He arranges them meticulously on a canvas placed in odd locations. He calls this an art composition.

4 Similarly, Gustav Mahler's first symphony's third movement is a parody of a children's song "Frêre Jacques," converted to a minor scale. It is the alteration of a well-known popular song into a dark passionate opus using a mapping system.

5 Heelan, P. offers an extensive survey on *Space-perception and the Philosophy of Science*, Berkeley: University of California Press, 1988. Also Lunenburg, R. in his paper "The Metric of Visual Space", *Journal of the Optical Society of America*, vol. 40, 1950, pp. 627–642, offers a description of hyperbolic space. A simulation of the mapping between physical and visual space has been implemented as a real-time computational application in Terzidis, K., "Experiments on Projection Systems", *ACADIA Quarterly*, vol. 16, no. 4, 1999, pp. 8–15.

6 For the latest (at this time) modeling techniques see Praun, E. *et al.*, "Consistent Mesh Parameterizations", and Biermann, H. *et al.* "Approximate Boolean Operations on Free-form Solids", both in Los Angeles: *ACM SIGGRAPH Proceedings*, New York: ACM Press, 2001, pp. 179–184 and 185–194 respectively.

7 One of the first theorists to identify and explore the idea of soft objects in architectural design was Marcos Novak. In his paper "Computational Compositions", *Computing in Design Education, ACADIA '88 Workshop Proceedings*, ed. P.J. Bancroft, Ann Arbor, University of Michigan, October 1988, Marcos identified the three important principles of digital architecture: (a) the replacement of the finite object by the variable object, (b) the idea of pluralism replacing singularity, and (c) the existence of equally accessible information. In his work, he explores the idea of architecture as process rather than output.

Chapter 2

Hybrid Form[1]

Morphing is a term used to describe a process in which an object changes its form gradually in order to obtain another form.[2] Morphing is a gradual transition that results in a marked change in the form's appearance, character, condition, or function. While the cinematic model of morphing involves screen-based apparent rather than actual or substantive changes on the form itself, the architectural implementation of morphing suggests geometrical and topological transitions. Such processes involve operations that affect the geometry of a form while preserving its topology. Morphing is the interconnection between seemingly disparate entities. In its dynamic stage, it is the struggle to connect the unconnected, dissimilar, unrelated, and unalike. In its static stage, morphing is the bond between the past and the present. It embodies a formal definition of *reminiscence* in its most primitive and primordial state.

The process of morphing differs from the biological process of *metamorphosis*. While metamorphosis is the change in the form, and often function, of an animal during normal development after the embryonic stage, morphing is a man-made, artificial process of mapping between often unrelated entities. The transformation of a maggot into an adult fly or a tadpole into a frog follows natural biological laws. In contrast, morphing follows artificial rules. It is the simulation of a mathematical interpolation. Thus, it appears to be a process of magic or sorcery and the effects may often look strange, awkward, or surprising.

Recent theories of form in architecture have focused on *topological geometry*. They refer to "smooth spaces described by continuous yet differentiated systems resulting from curvilinear sensibilities that are capable of complex deformations in response to programmatic structural, economic, aesthetic, political and contextual influences".[3] A topological transformation, or a *homeomorphism*, of one figure into another, is described as a bi-univocal and bi-continuous correspondence between the points of the respective figures maintaining the connection and vicinity of the points of the figure.[4] Topological operations involve folding, stretching, and compressing but not tearing or cutting. Topology may be regarded as the unifying force that preserves the integrity of an indefinitely changing geometry.

In this context, architectural morphing preserves the structural integrity of the objects involved, that is, an object changes into another object as a single entity. A cube, for instance, may be gradually transformed into a pyramid. From the viewer's point of view, there are always two objects: *the original (or source)*, to which transformation is applied, and the *destination object (or target)*, which is the object one will get at the final step of the transformation. However, theoretically, there is only one object, which is transformed from one state (original) into another (destination). This object combines characteristics of both of the parent objects involved in the transformation and is called a *hybrid object*. This object is actually composed of the topology of the one object and the geometry of the other. It is an object in disguise. Although it is topologically identical to the one parent it resembles the geometry of the other parent.

The operation of morphing consists basically of the selection of two objects and the assignment of a number of in-between transitional steps. The first object then transforms into the second in steps. The essence of such a transformation resides not in the destination form but rather in the intermediate phases these transformations pass through and in the extrapolations, which go beyond the final form. It is the transitional continuity of a form that progresses through a series of evolutionary stages.

Interpolation is a method for estimating values that lie between two known values. The hybrid object derives its structure from its parents through formal interpolations. While it is easy to derive hybrid children from isomorphic parents, a challenge arises for heteromorphic parents. In an isomorphic transformation, a one-to-one correspondence applies between the elements of the two parent sets, such that the result of an operation on elements of one set corresponds to the result of the analogous operation on their images in the other set. In the case of heteromorphism, the lack of homogeneity among the parents leads necessarily to a selective process of omissions and inclusion of elements between the two sets. The guiding principle in this mapping process is the preservation of the topological and geometrical properties of the hybrid object. For instance, in the case of a square mapped to a triangle, the addition of a fourth point to the triangle preserves the topology of the square, but its disguised location preserves the geometrical appearance of the triangle.

What makes morphing problematic for architects is that they have maintained an ethics of accumulative progression during the design process. Because of the artificial nature of design, architects traditionally follow a bottom-up approach. Iakov Chernikov and other constructivists, for example, elaborated on the combination of forms, using the basic concepts of "constructive combinations", such as amalgamation, combination, assemblage, conjugation, penetration, embracing, mounting, inte-

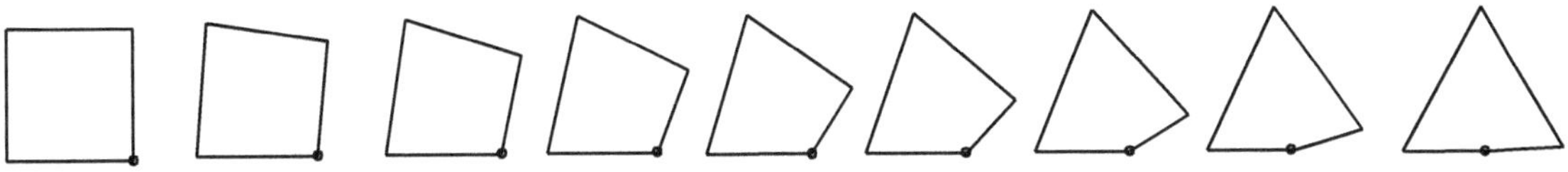

2.1
In the case of a square mapped to a triangle, the addition of a fourth point to the triangle preserves the topology of the square, but its disguised location preserves the geometrical appearance of the triangle

grating, coupling, interlacing, clamping, linking and so on, both statically and dynamically, using hard or soft materials. These concepts constitute a Boolean design language, one having the advantage of combining forms in a manner familiar to architects.

By contrast, morphing is a process of homogeneous transition. No elements are added or subtracted from the scene. Hybrid design is an alternative to the incremental design approach, which starts with components and builds toward increasing complexity, as, for instance, building blocks. Instead, it starts with complex models or constructs, which get compared and transformed from one into the other. This allows an architect to impose a new condition or configuration on an existing design, create an evolution from one design to another, or explore the implications of contrasting design positions.

The process of creation, in nature, is extremely complicated. Yet from a formal point of view, the form of the child is a manifestation of the formal characteristics of both parents involved. The formal character of the hybrid object is derived from the features of its parents. The shape and form of the child combines both of the parents' features and yet it has its own identity, which is a unique blending of the two parents. The morphological value of the hybrid is in its subtle reminiscence of its parent. At the same time, the hybrid has its own identity, which is often stronger than that of its own parents.

Traditionally in architecture, skeletal shapes are used as abstract organizational schemes for the analysis or synthesis of buildings. These gestalt shapes are commonly known as *"partis"*. They are symbolic configurations or patterns of elements so unified as a whole that their properties cannot be derived from a simple summation of their parts. The formal value of these shapes is tremendous since they not only describe the organizational structure of the building but also express certain archetypal attributes associated with the theme of the building.[5] In partis, enclosure, balance, direction, rhythm, hierarchy, or symmetry are depicted through the use of Euclidean shapes and geometric configurations. A parti is not only a descriptive underlay but also a symbolic manifestation. As the hybrid form strives to express itself through its parents' identity, a challenge arises in the selection of the parents. If partis are used as parents, then hybridization will occur between these archetypal shapes. The process of interpolation becomes the connecting bridge between interpretations. For instance, morphing a foursquare parti into a circle is not about four shapes that merge into one but rather about the concept of hard, sharp and equilateral changing into the soft, smooth, and concentric. The more the contrast between the parents, the higher the chances are for the hybrid form to juxtapose, cross-pollinate, and emerge.

The dominant mode for discussing the notion of time has been that of a linear progression, where events happen in a sequential fashion. The notions of "before" and "after" imply direction and polarity between two points of reference. Time is often depicted as a line that starts in the negative infinity and ends in the positive infinity. The problem with this model is that it assumes that every moment in time is of identical importance and that the exact same event in time never occurs twice. This is quite contrary to personal experience of time where some moments are more important than others and events do seem to repeat themselves quite often. In contrast to the linear model, if time were defined by a curve, then progression would occur as a rotational interpolation, allowing the exaggeration of certain moments and the reduction of others. In addition, instead of assuming that "before" will always be followed by "after", a circular definition of time may lead to the oxymoron of "before" occurring after "after".[6] Rather than defining time along a line, a circle or a closed shape may be used instead. The result may be surprising and unexpected, yet closer to our perception of time as a reoccurring phenomenon. With this technique, progression from one state to another is weighted, oscillated, and iterated.

Change is a phenomenon perceptible by the senses and, as such, it is prone to interpretation. Observation of change of form is associated with its physical growth, development, or decay. However, change itself is a constant measure. If everything changes at the same rate, the differential distance is constant, preventing change from being conceived. In contrast, sudden, abrupt, and unexpected are characteristics of change, whereas constant, smooth, and predicted are not. This implies that form itself can depict change through its own rate of deformation. If time consists of a succession of discrete instants, then change can be conceived as overlapping or unfolding deformations. In architecture, the expression of change is by nature implicit since buildings cannot change physically. The impression of change, however, is often depicted by architects through overlapping or unfolding deformations using transparent layers or progressive slices.[7] The problem with this method is that it is too literal, leaving little space for visual interpretation. In contrast, implicit methods make use of the value of visual connotation so change is expressed through its inductive presence. The hybrid form is an implicit form that suggests a dynamic blending of genetic forces superimposed by the subtle reminiscence of its creators.

One of the main differences of morphing, as it compares to deformation, is in the *duality* of its identity. Deformation is understood as a change relative to an initial state. As a point of reference, an archetype is needed to assess the degree of deformation. However, as the deformation persists, form reaches a threshold beyond which it becomes "unrecognizable", meaning that it is impossible to associate it with its pivotal archetype. That is not the case in morphing. In fact, as the interpolation persists, the hybrid form oscillates between the identifiable shapes of its parents, allowing comparisons to be made at any point. This formal atavistic property is very important, as it becomes a means of expressing change through form itself, and not through juxtaposition. The duality of its identity is a unique compositional and unifying theme of the hybrid form.

2.2

A square is mapped to a triangle. While certain mappings appear to be more "natural" (above) than others (below), every mapping is a valid transformation between the two parent sets

Morphing can be conceived as a unifying, but also as a diversifying process. Hybrid represents the state of form where the ancestors' features are unified and passed through the next generations. However, during the evolution, special personalities may appear: certain hybrid forms that stand out. The two linked principles that are central to the formal interpretation of hybrid forms are (1) the resemblance to its parents and (2) the autonomy of the resemblance. The second principle may seem to be a contradictory statement, but, in reality, it refers to the special condition of overlapping personalities: when something has its own personality and yet reminds us of something else; where similarity, resemblance, and alikeness evolve into the independent, self-reliant, and autonomous. It is the point in the history of evolution when new strong identities are born. It is that point in a pedigree that stands out, redefines, and diversifies the process of evolution.

In the interpolation process, a mapping applies between the elements of the two parent sets, such that the elements of the one set correspond to their images in the other set. Practically, multiple mappings can be constructed between the elements of the two sets. For every element in one set, any element of the image set can be mapped. While certain mappings appear to be more "natural" than others, every mapping is a valid transformation between the two parent sets. A *mutation* is an unexpected alteration to the hybrid's structure resulting in the creation of a new character or trait, not found in the parental type. Mutation is an alteration that occurs during the creation process and certainly not after. Since the creation of hybrid forms involves parents and mappings, a mutation may be defined as an "abnormal" mapping. The value of mutation is important since it represents a deviation from the ordinary, the common and the predictable. It is about exploration of alternatives, missing links, and new traits. A mutation has a high formal value, as it is associated with controversial interpretations. What appears to be a monster may also be worshipped as a god. In the history of architecture, deviations from the common practice have often been regarded as landmarks of progression.

The term *extrapolation* is used to describe the method of inferring or estimating by extending or projecting known information. By assuming that estimated

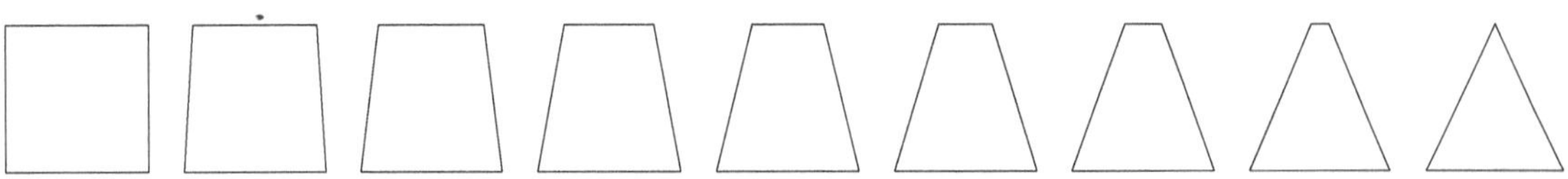

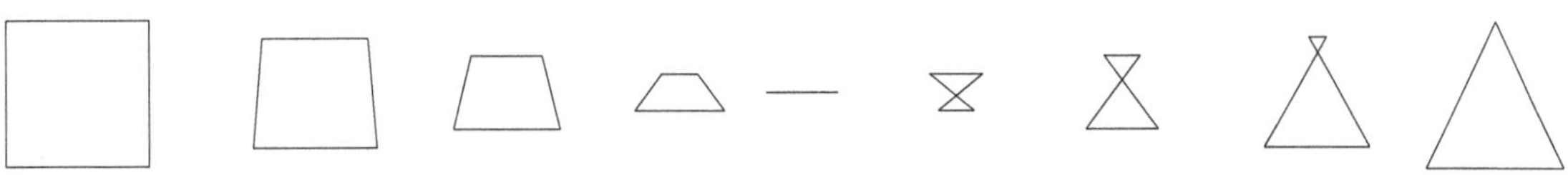

values follow logically from known values, extrapolation estimates values outside a known range from values within a known range. Extrapolation is similar to interpolation. The method is the same, but the range of jurisdiction is the opposite. Because extrapolation is a logical extension of a known process, its formal value is not understood instantly. While interpolation is about middle ground, average, transition, and oscillation, extrapolation is about inversion, reversion, extension, and extremeness. Extrapolation represents a gateway to infinity. It is the starting point of inverted logic where the one parent is present through its mirror image. The extrapolated form is still a hybrid; it may appear awkward, and yet it is perfectly consistent within the morphing rules. In fact, the child of two extrapolated parents is identical to that of two normal parents.

An interesting twist on morphing is that of *cross programming* or *cloning*. Cloning is a term used to express a form that copies or closely resembles another in appearance or function.[8] It is based on interpretation and as such it needs to be associated with an archetype. It is an implicit method of alteration based on behavior rather than form. For instance, a church converted to a mosque, such as St Sophia in Istanbul, or a mosque converted into a church, such as in Cordoba, Spain, are examples of architectural cloning. Cloning is about pretension, ostentation, double meaning, form, and content.

If architecture is to approach morphing as an alternative design method, its design technologies should also incorporate factors of time and change. The power of computation is in its ability to extend the human mind and set the ground for experimentation into the unknown. The processes of interpolation and extrapolation are essentially mathematical processes and as such they can be codified into quan-

2.3
The child C of two extrapolated parents 'A' and 'B' is identical to that of two normal parents

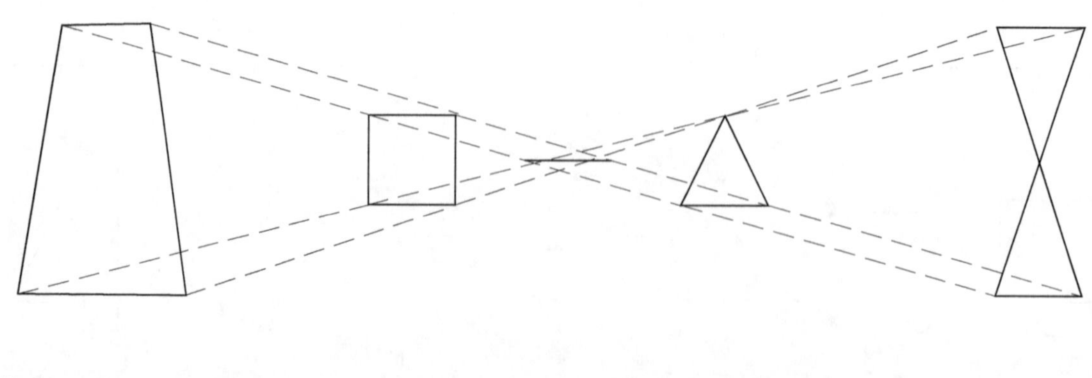

titative methods. In contrast, manipulations, evaluations, and combinations of these processes are qualitative processes and as such can be handled by the architect.

Morphing is a powerful formal device that embodies one of architecture's most existential struggles: to express and identify itself through its own form. An almost unique characteristic of architecture is that it is both dynamic and static. It is dynamic when viewed as the design process which has its roots in historical precedents of culture and the arts and which manipulates entities which are typically of an elastic character. It becomes static when it has to freeze at a certain state so that it may be built. In other words, architecture is static when viewed through individual buildings. It is dynamic when these buildings are viewed as instances of a continuum, which derives from the past and projects into the future. In its dynamic stage, morphing involves transition, progress, continuity, interpolation and evolution. In its static stage, it involves expression, connotation, mixing, combination, and bonding. Surprisingly, in architecture morphing is not about change, but instead about a particular moment in time when the past and the future overlap within the same form. It involves transitional continuity and dynamic stasis. The identifiable characteristics of morphing are both unified multiplicity and intermediate distinctiveness.

The process of morphing is not necessarily a linear interpolation of all components at the same time. *Orchestration* is a term used to describe the actions of selecting, assigning, directing, and evaluating the performance of objects, which participate in the morphing process. Transformations can happen concurrently or at different pace. The result is a *truly dynamic design space*, the behavior of which becomes the responsibility of the architect. As in an orchestral performance, the architect/composer selects a number of objects to participate, assigns the proper paths and momentum for each one, and then directs the performance through time, form, and color.[9]

One of the key themes of today's technologies is *integration*. From cars and computers to social groups and corporations, a great deal of effort is spent on how to connect, integrate, merge, and blend into new entities. New entities are produced every day that are the result of integration or merging of other subentities.[10] From merger names and company logos, to blending racial groups and multipurpose architectural buildings, we constantly experience a trend toward a new type of aesthetics, that of *blending*. One of the side-effects of integration is its formal manifestation. Morphing can play a key role in this trend. At its conceptual level, morphing is understood as the integration of tangible entities over time. However, theoretically, it is a process of interpolation and as such it can be applied to almost any set or pattern, such as words, narratives, sounds, shapes, or images.

While many disciplines can benefit from the morphing process, language is the most prominent since it embodies the most universal, extensible, flexible, and symbolic system for defining new ideas. The logical analysis of language as a method of inquiry is one that regards statements as meaningful only if they are either logically analytic or theoretically verifiable in experience. The merging of words in the English dictionary – that is, the process of combining parts of words, words, or phrases into new ones – involves the blending of linguistic meanings. Following on the logic of formal morphing, experimentation with language and semantics can address the dynamic nature that is inherent in modern language. New words and meanings are being created constantly by the blending of contemporary technology with social distinctions and our human understanding of the relationship between ourselves and the world around us. In this context, morphing methods can be used to create new hybrid names *for yet to be defined concepts*. An example of such experimentation is crossing the boundaries of an English-based dictionary with regional expressions, street jargon, or even other languages. Driven by a genetically based algorithmic process, new kinds of meaning and form arise from words whose parents come from seemingly disparate regions, for example from a ghetto of Los Angeles and Japan.[11] Experimental systems using computer science, mathematical algorithms and genetic processes can prompt the blending of existing words into new hybrid gestalts *for yet to be designed forms*.

A challenging point is the fact that this new aesthetics is about the unknown, the unpredictable, and the unforeseeable. It requires the cooperation of two brains: that of the human and the computer, for without one another it is impossible to plan or execute the hybrid objects. Most of all, such hybrid objects lead to the creation of computational schemes, which are available for experimentation, analysis or play across disciplines. The hybrid object contributes to our understanding of aesthetics and creates a new dimension of how it may change our perception. It also brings up a social point: who is the creator? How will it change our perception if science and mathematics can mold into the creative process?

Notes

1 A shorted version of this chapter can be found in Terzidis, K., "Hybrid Form", *Design Issues*, Cambridge, MA. MIT Press, Winter Issue 2003, vol. 19, no. 1, pp. 57–61.

2 An extensive introduction to morphing and warping for computer graphics is given by Gomez, J. (ed.), *Warping and Morphing of Graphical Objects*, San Francisco, CA: Morgan Kaufmann Publishers, 1997.

3 This is Greg Lynn's interpretation of Gilles Deleuze's *The Fold: Leibniz and the Baroque* and Rene Thom's catastrophe diagrams. See Lynn, G., "Architectural Curvilinearity", in *Architecture and Science*, G. Di Cristina, ed. Chichester: Wiley Academy, 2001, p. 27.

4 See Di Cristina, G., "The Topological Tendency in Architecture", in ibid., p. 7.

5 Handbooks such as Francis D.K. Ching's *Architecture: Form, Space and Order*, New York: John Wiley, 1996, and Roger H. Clark and Michael Pause's *Precedents in Architecture*, New York: Wiley, 1996 are also useful sources for establishing a foundation of architectural abstraction, a foundation, like all foundations, to build upon, to exceed.

6 The movie *Memento* by Jonathan and Christopher Nolan (2001) challenges the traditional concept of linear progression and plays with time, narrative, and audience perception. Time is being used as a non-linear, inverted, and syncopated phenomenon.

7 Thomas Leeser manifests spatially the liquidity of processes in his VERTego diagrams (see Thomas Leeser, *Invertigo* Assemblage 16 Mit Press: Cambridge MA. pp. 48–65 1991). Also Greg Lynn, in

his design for the Cardiff Bay Opera House, uses progressive slicing to depict change through juxtaposition (see Greg Lynn and Jesse Reiser, *Computer Animisms (Two Designs for the Cardiff Bay Opera House)* Assemblage 26: MIT Press: Cambridge MA, pp. 8–37 April 1995).

8 An interesting example of expression cloning can be found in *SIGGRAPH 2001 Conference Proceedings*, New York: ACM Press, 2001, pp. 277–286. The authors, Jun-yong Noh *et al.*, mix archetypal faces with expressions from other personalities to explore the subtle implications of superimposing the familiar with the unexpected.

9 One of the first attempts to use morphing in architecture was reported by Terzidis in 1989. Its intention was to introduce the hybrid object as an architectural parti. It is worth noticing that the word "morphing" was invented later. See Terzidis, K., "Transformational Design", *New Ideas and Directions for the 1990s, ACADIA Proceedings*, ed. C.I. Yesios, Gainsville, FL. University of Florida, 1989.

10 Think of the following newly created words–concepts: edutainment, infomercial, inforum, bikecology, verizon, microsoft, imagineering, etc.

11 An elegant way to do this sort of processing is a technique called a *Markov chain algorithm.* If we imagine the input as a sequence of overlapping phrases, the algorithm divides each phrase into two parts, a multi-word *prefix* and a single *suffix* word that follows the prefix. A Markov chain algorithm emits output phrases by randomly choosing the suffix that follows the prefix, according to the statistics of the original text.

Chapter 3

Kinetic Form

Kinetic is a term used to describe a situation related to, or produced by, motion. Motion is the act or process of changing position or place over time. While motion involves time as a measurement of change, the definition of form itself does not involve time. As a result, "kinetic form" is not a contradiction but rather an extension to the notion of form as a motionless boundary.[1] It is about the idea that perpetual succession is not only conceived directly through physical motion but also indirectly through formal expression.

The term kinetic enjoys a long history in relation to the arts, particularly and most recently as it was used in the kinetic art movement of the 1950s and 1960s. As Frank Popper[2] explains, kinetic art

> covers all two of three-dimensional works in actual movement, including machines, mobiles and projections, whether controlled or uncontrolled; it also covers works in virtual movement, that is to say, in which the spectator's eye responds quite clearly to the physical stimuli.

In architecture, the idea of motion is often represented as an abstract formal configuration that implies relationships of cause and effect. Displacement, reduction, suppression, amputation, miniaturization, augmentation, addition, extension, amplification, substitution, absence, contamination, dissociation, dislocation, friction, and penetration are just a few of the terms used by architects to express motion and change. The dominant model for representing motion in architecture has been that of the imposition of physical or formal forces that shape the evolution of form. More than ever now, through the use of applied physics and computation, design space can become a dynamic simulation environment for the exploration of physical forces on material forms.

The problem with such a physics-based design model is that form is not always conceived as made out of matter. In fact, form is rather an abstract entity that possesses certain geometric characteristics. For instance, dots on a piece of paper may imply a shape not because they are made out of ink but because of their geometric relationships. The attachment of material qualities constrains the behavior of form and restricts the designer's imagination. In contrast, the lack of materiality liberates the form from its constraints and introduces behaviors closer to intuition rather than perception.

In Euclidean geometry, form is conceived as the result of a system of abstract relationships. Forms represent idealized versions of conceptual patterns and not perceivable objects. The formal relationships that define primitive shapes are based on the condition of *stasis*, or balance of conceptual forces. Euclidean primitives describe special conditions where an equilibrium state has been obtained. A circle is not about roundness but rather about the equal distance of points from a central point. The ellipse, which in Greek means *omission*, reflects a "failure" to obtain the equilateral equilibrium of a circle.

Motion, in a way, negates the Euclidean concept of stasis and introduces potentiality. Distance is associated with time allowing form to set itself in motion. While time is the measure of change, its definition poses a problem. The Aristotelian definition of time is based on the notions of "before" and "after". Motion can be perceived through the senses by comparing the change of "after" compared to that of "before". This assumption is antithetical to that of Euclidean continuity because it introduces two discrete consecutive instances of time. If a line is composed of infinite points and no measurable distance between two consecutive points, time should also be structured similarly. Zeno's paradoxes were based on the idea of continuous time and therefore the inability to insert a moment between moments.[3] As a result, a new notion, that of *infinitesimal* distance, had to be invented, to allow "before" and "after" to be separated by an extremely finite distance. In that context, form starts its journey of motion at the moment when two infinitesimal moments connect.

Continuity is the state or quality of being uninterrupted in time, sequence, substance, or extent. The notion of continuous is abstract and theoretical. While, in appearance, time and space appear to be continuous, it can be claimed that practically nothing is really continuous. If time and space are composed of finite elements, then there must be a disruption between two neighboring elements.

The term "resolution" refers to the fineness of detail that can be distinguished in a discrete pattern. Practically, there is no such thing as infinite resolution. From a theoretical point of view, analytic methods assume the integration of finite elements into a whole, as infinitesimally small elements form a continuous blending. Yet this logic applies more to the senses, specifically vision, rather than the brain. Through vision, continuity is interpreted as a trend which when it reaches the threshold of invisibility is assumed to continue thereafter. In contrast, logical consistency is a principle of human thought that denies continuity when an inconsistency occurs, regardless of the visible trend.

Continuity and discontinuity are two terms that are often conceived as opposites. In fact, deflection, inflection, bending, deviation, and disturbance are forms of discontinuity or continuity, yet none amount to an abrupt break, gap, or pause. For instance, a speed bump is a disruption in the flow of traffic, yet it represents neither discontinuity nor continuity. Zeno's paradoxes dealt with the inability to demarcate the limit that separates the continuous from the discontinuous.

In differential geometry, form is being represented as a function of time. Derivative is the change in direction of a point traveling along a curve when the time lapse between "before" and "after" is *almost* zero. The purpose of this geometry is to study changes in the properties of forms within infinitesimal moments using the methods of calculus. Curves and surfaces are differentiated in different directions to reveal the behavior of motion along a path. Interestingly, the resulting Euclidean forms represent motion instead of stasis.

While the goal of motion may be immovability, the goal of kinetic form is to express perpetual motion through its immovable structure. In architecture, physical motion, other than in doors, windows, elevators, or escalators, is not present in buildings. In fact, the form and structure of the average building suggests stability, steadiness, sturdiness, and immobility. While motion may suggest instability, agility, or uncertainty, it also suggests change, anticipation, vigor, and liveliness. The illusion of motion, often described as "frozen movement", has been argued to have a high architectural value.[4] It illustrates the immense forces of what architects have often been talking about as "punctured volume", "compressed planes", "interpenetrating spaces", or "agitated surfaces". In that context, frozen movement expresses an almost unique characteristic of architecture: that it is both dynamic and static. It is dynamic when viewed as the design process which has its roots in historical precedents of culture and the arts and which manipulates entities that are typically of an elastic character. It becomes static when it has to freeze at a certain state so that it may be built.

Observations

The perception of motion is relative; if everything is moving at the same speed, motion is not perceivable. Thus, a point of reference is needed to contrast the moving from the static. From a visual standpoint, stasis can be represented by balance and motion by direction. The juxtaposition of a balanced organization next to a directional configuration may suggest flow and motion.

Superimposition is the act of laying or placing something on or over something else. Overlays of transparent or translucent forms can play a key role in expressing motion by the use of concentric wrinkles or shivering jelly-like behavior. Their

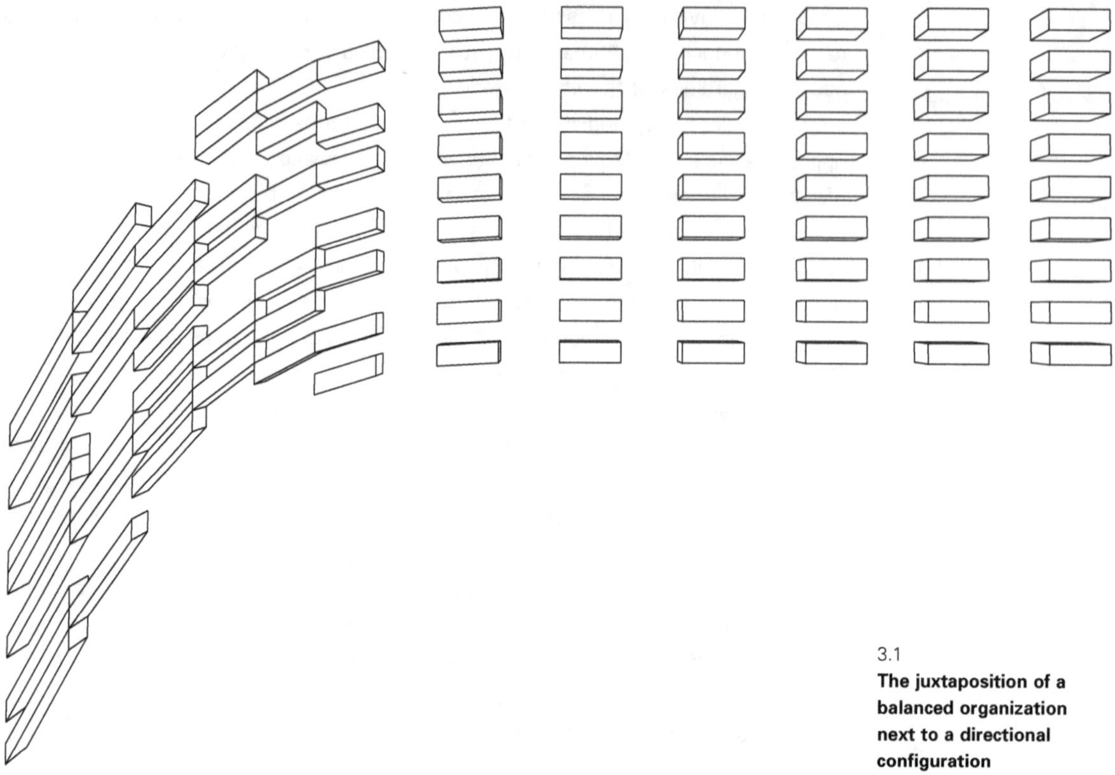

3.1
The juxtaposition of a balanced organization next to a directional configuration

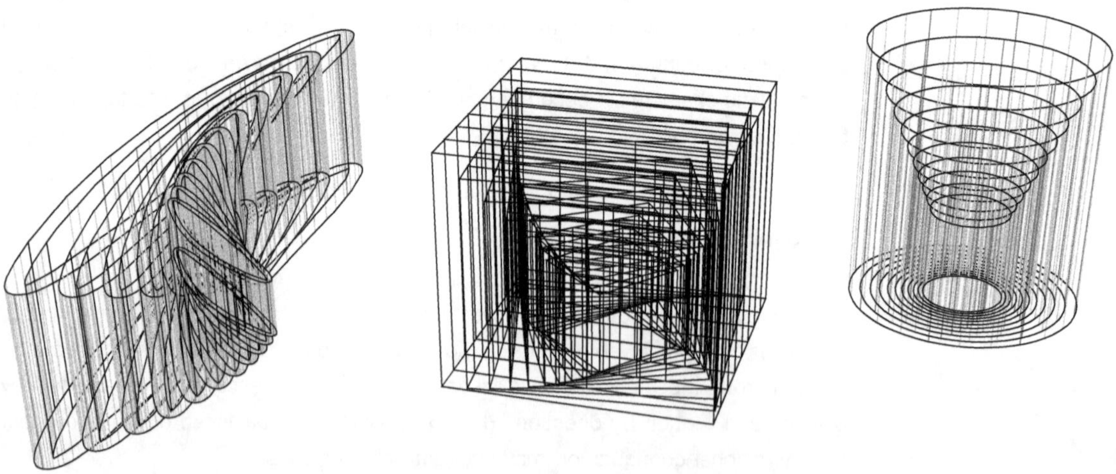

3.2
Superimposition

suggestive power can be found in their ability to represent overlapping moments within the same form.

Sequential juxtaposition is a configuration where a series of changes to a form are laid out in a sequential fashion. While its expressive value for representing motion is mainly based on linear interpretation, it differs from superimposition. Sequential juxtaposition is about evolution, continuity, tracing, and formation, whereas superimposition is about introversion, internal disturbance, agitation, and agility.

Friction is a force that resists the relative motion or tendency to such motion of two bodies in contact. Friction, as well as inertia, expresses the resistance of matter to sudden change. Both are perceived as motion when they are associated with matter and force.

Deformation can also be associated with friction. The shaping forces of fluid dynamics are suggestive of a form's attempt to flow through another medium.

Adhesion, stickiness, resistance, and sluggishness are qualities of matter that suggest resistance to motion. Their suggestive power can be found in the fact that they imply motion through their negation to initiate it.

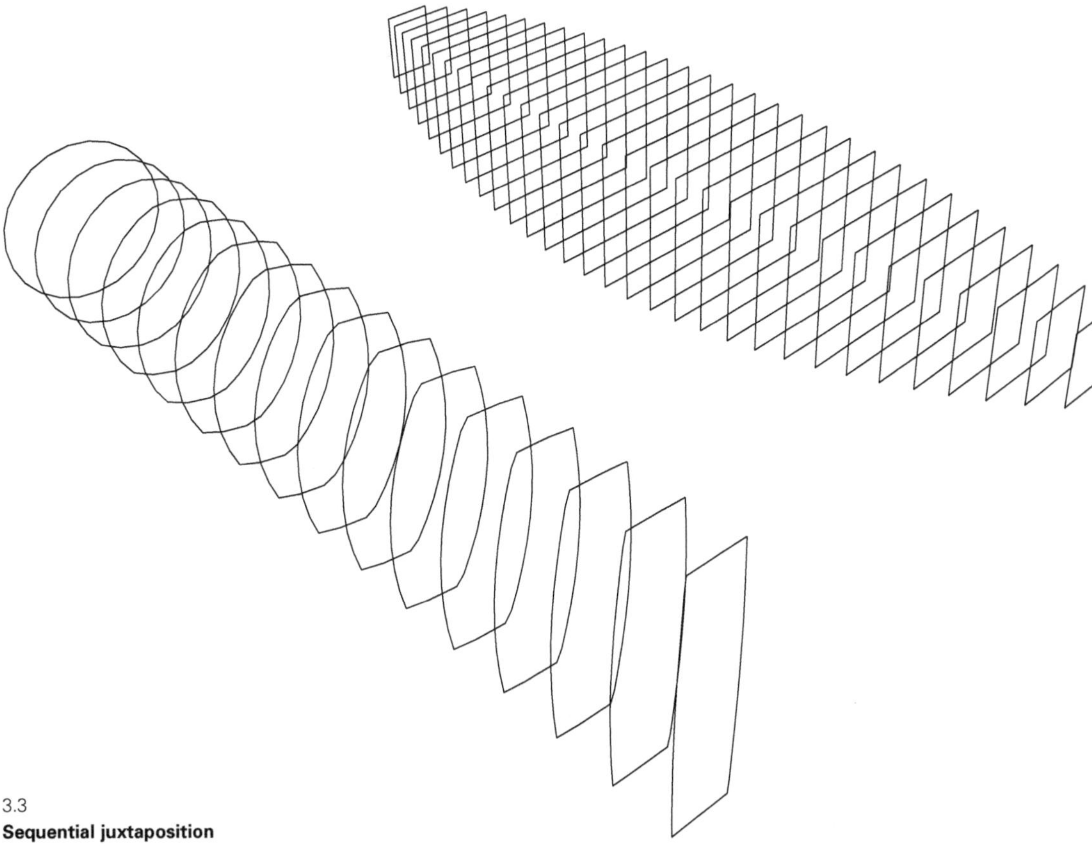

3.3
Sequential juxtaposition

Absence is the state of being away. Subtraction is the act of taking something away. They both imply change since something was detached or disappeared. Absence is also interpreted as lack of desire. It is often interpreted as the desire to see something that is not there.

Aftereffect is an effect following its cause after some delay, especially a delayed or prolonged physiological or psychological response to a stimulus. It is the result that implies the cause. It is "after" that suggests "before". The behavior of finite elements shaped by dynamic or catastrophic forces may imply change, disturbance, shock, or disarray.

While physical motion is a result of the application of kinetic forces, the visual impression of motion does not necessarily follow from the laws of physics. "Before" and "after" can be mixed, reversed, or implied in ways that contradict or negate physical laws and yet be fully understood by the viewer as motion. Cartoons and caricatures are examples of such psychological illusion: phones that, when they ring, become larger in size, cars that elongate as they accelerate, objects surrounded with lines to imply motion, spacecraft with phonetics such as "vroom" behind them, and so on. Figure 3.9 may be understood as the disturbance of a ball against a lineup of blocks, although this is actually impossible because the ball has not collided yet with the blocks.

The Heracliteian concept of motion is mixed with that of stability. A river, for example, is conceived as one thing and yet every moment it is not the same since different and again different waters would flow over one's feet. Motion can also be regarded as a phenomenon and as such can be suggested to the viewer. Instead of presenting movement as a literal representation of a progressive pattern, a more subtle representation can be used instead. The notion of tacit information and its suggestive value can be instrumental in implying movement without the actual moving element. Through metaphor or analogy certain facts can be inferred without actually presenting the whole story. Waterfalls without water or the tip of an iceberg are suggestive, implicit, and connotative notions involving tacit information. Instead of giving out the whole picture, a connecting-the-dots interpretation engages the viewer to participate in the visual composition.

A fugue is a polyphonic composition in which themes or a theme stated successively by a number of voices in imitation is developed contrapuntally. In music, variations of scale and pitch can be successively superimposed to form an elevated, exalted, accumulative, glorifying, and apotheotic build-up. Similarly, schemes or configurations of volumes can be transformed, deformed and superimposed progressively to construct formal build-ups. In architecture, churches, temples, concert halls, and cinema-theaters use such build-up schemes to introduce the viewers to successive steps of ritual processes that lead to a final place–destination.

The study of kinetic form can benefit tremendously from the use of computational tools. Simulated dynamic environments, complex deformations, rendering techniques, and mathematical surfaces are some of the many processes and mechanisms available today for exploration and experimentation. While tools

3.4
Friction

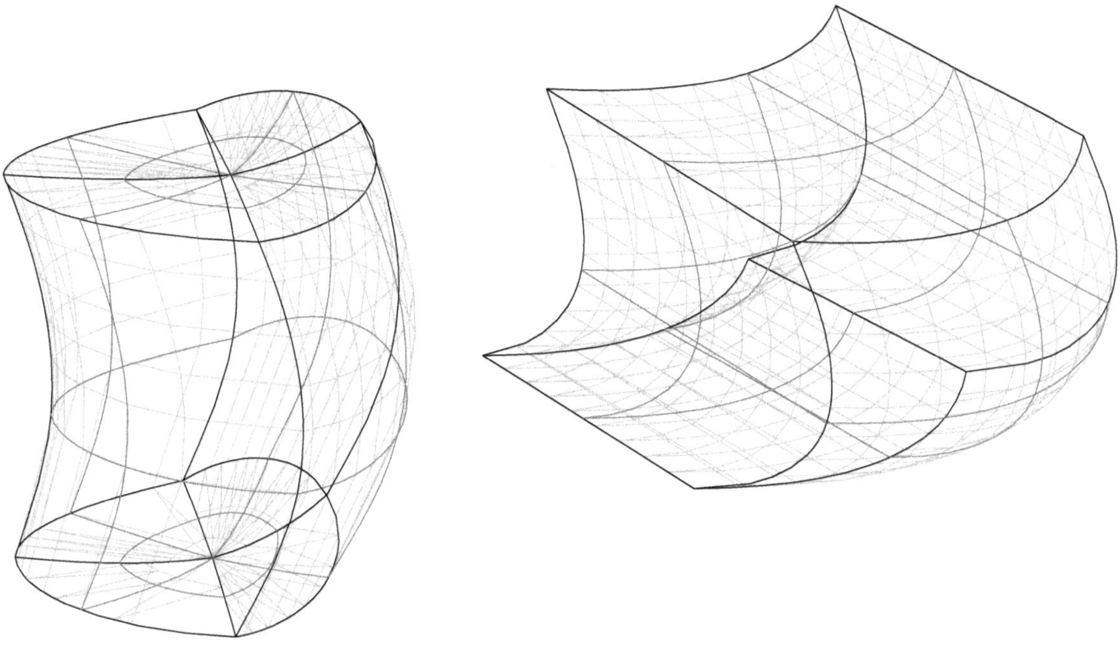

3.5
Deformation

are not any smarter than the hands that use them, computational methods offer a glimpse into a world of wonder, play, surprise, and imagination.

Imagine a design space where all is in motion. A variety of elements, either of a geometrical form, such as primitives, or of a symbolic form signifying a memory of the past, are paraded and can be selected and/or operated by a designer who orchestrates the event. As organizational structures are introduced, they are executed in a continuous mode and in a way such that all the in-between stages are transparent and become part of the compositional experience. Processes may be reversed individually or in groups, applied at different velocities, or interrupted and redirected. The result is a *moving image*, the behavior of which becomes the

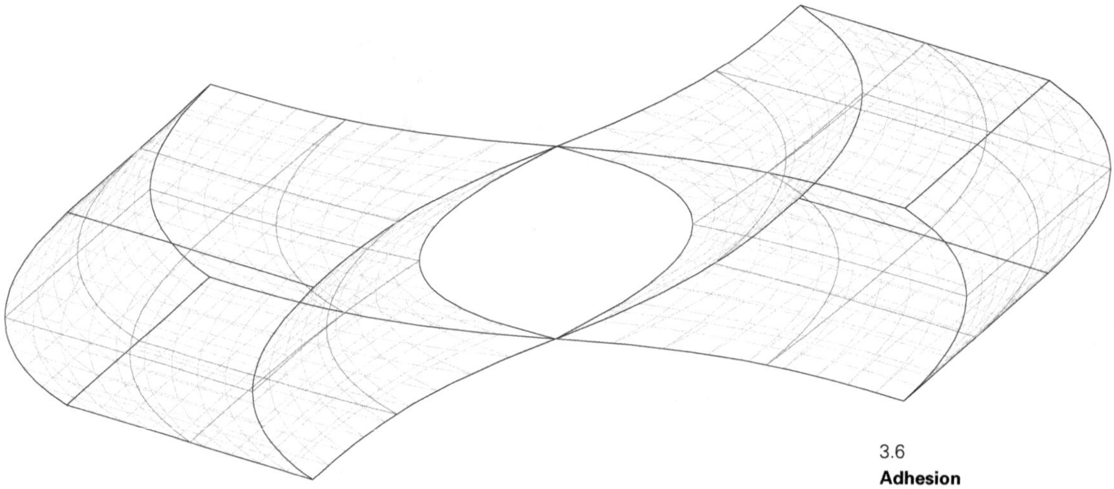

3.6
Adhesion

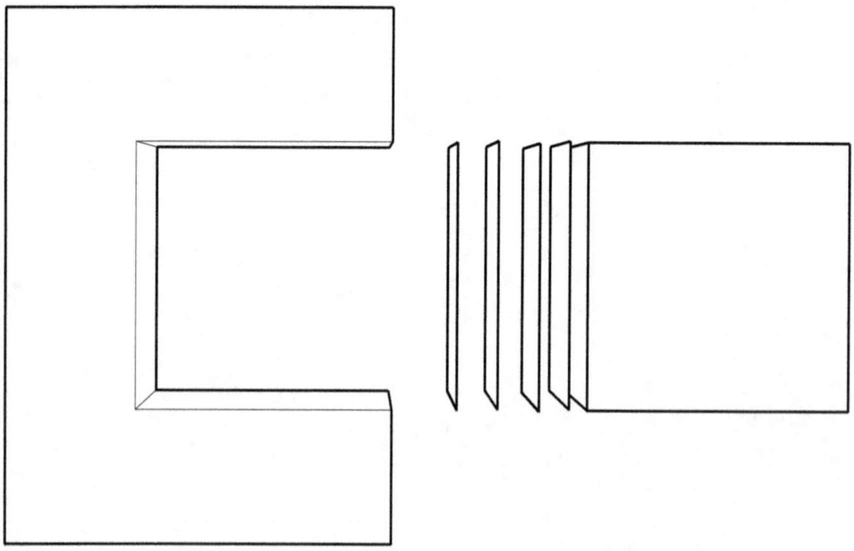

3.7
Absence

responsibility of the designer. As in an orchestra performance, the architect/composer selects a number of objects to participate, assigns the proper transformation paths and speeds, and then directs the performance through time, form and color.

Kandinsky dreamed of "a great city built according to all the rules of architecture and then suddenly shaken by a force that defies all calculation."[5] This dream sums up the double aspiration of architecture and architectural theory today and the double challenge of computational design. On the one hand we have the ability to design according to all the rules of architecture, a vast storehouse of accumulated compositional knowledge, on the other hand the ability to shake the rules, reconsider them, dislocate them, reinvent them, play.

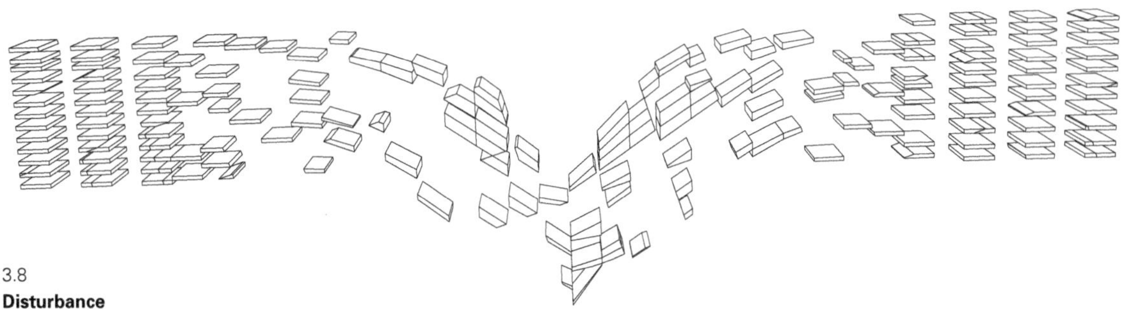

3.8
Disturbance

3.9
Visual impression of motion

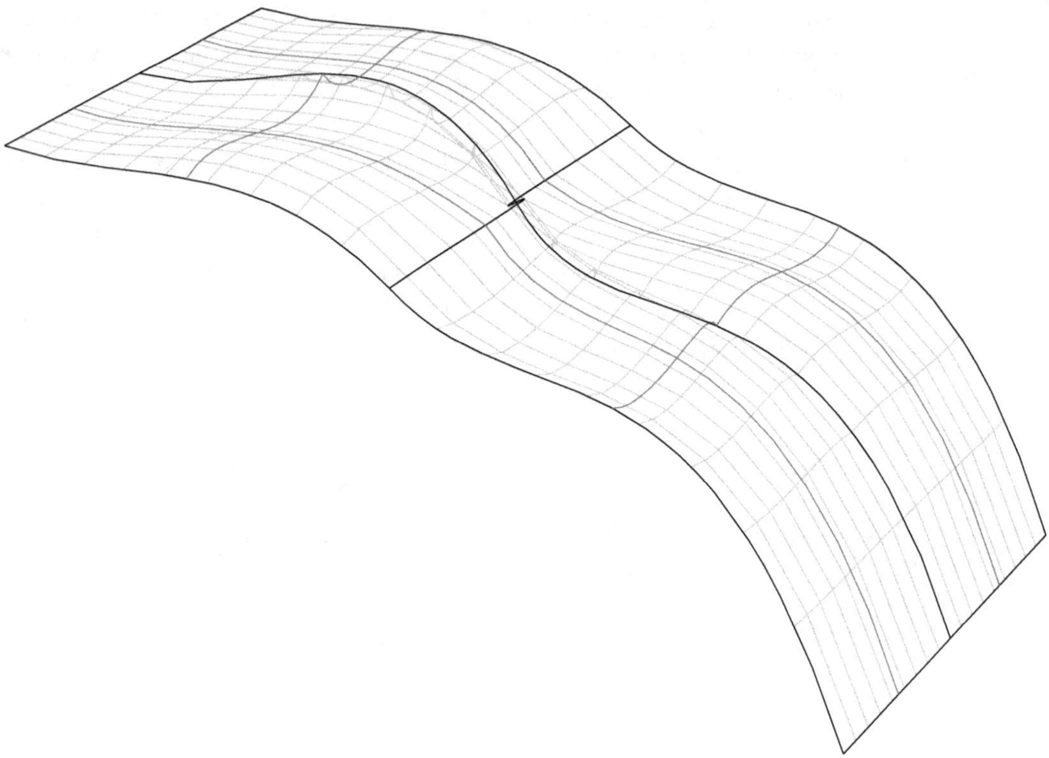

The traditional process of creating architecture thus becomes dislocated, and a new condition of design, perhaps called meta-architecture, is in view. The past theories of order thus may be seen as a final flourish at the end of an era of things, and the substantive difference between our time and the past is clearly seen in the transition to a new era of manipulating knowledge using high-level abstractions and nested systems of relations, rather than particular objects.[6] The architect of the past is seen as the virtuoso performer. The future architect may become the composer of symphonies in form, space, and color.

3.10
Texture

Notes

1 Aristotle in *Physics* refers to "place" as the innermost motionless boundary of what contains, whereas "time" is the number of motions in respect to before and after.

2 See Popper, Frank, *Origins and Development of Kinetic Art*, trans. Stephen Bann, New York: New York Graphic Society, 1968. Also see Popper, Frank, *Art of the Electronic Age*, London: Thames and Hudson, 1993, and Malina, F.J. (ed.) *Kinetic Art: Theory and Practice, Selections from the Journal* Leonardo, New York: Dover, 1974.

3 On the one hand Zeno can argue that the sum 1/2 + 1/4 + 1/8 + . . . never actually reaches 1, but more perplexing to the human mind is the attempt to sum 1/2 + 1/4 + 1/8 + . . . backwards. Before traversing a unit distance we must get to the middle, but before getting to the middle we must get

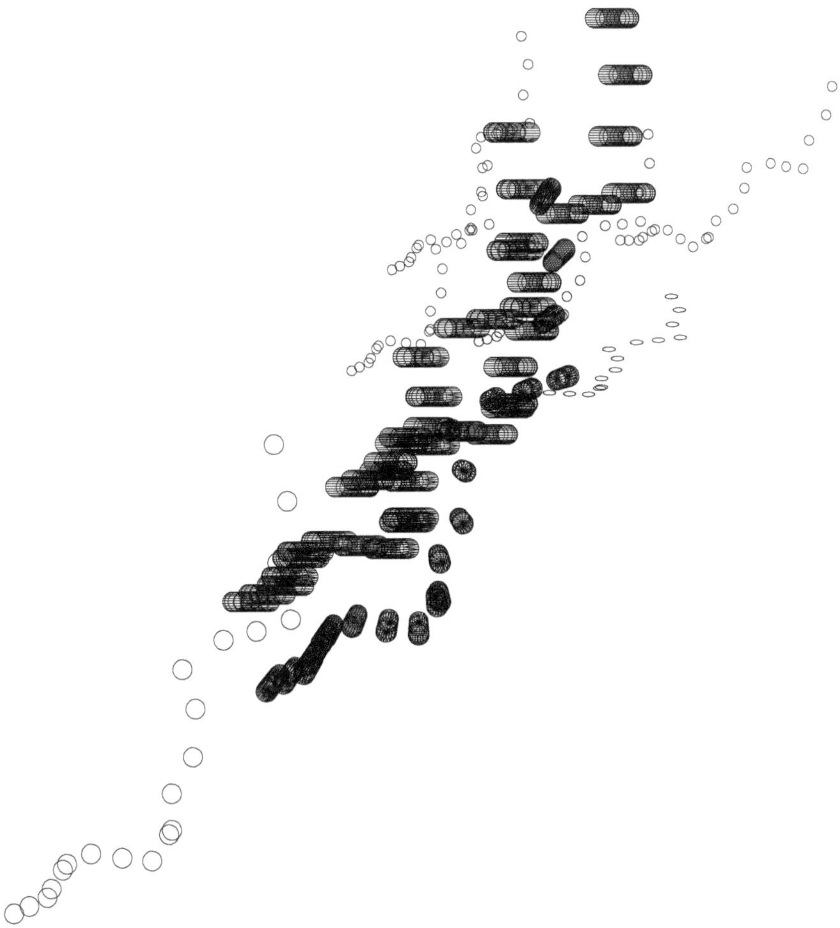

3.11
Combined formations

1/4 of the way, but before we get 1/4 of the way we must reach 1/8 of the way, etc. This argument makes us realize that we can never get started, since we are trying to build up this infinite sum from the "wrong" end.

Vlastos points out that if we use the standard mathematical formula for velocity we have v = s/t, where s is the distance traveled and t is the time taken. If we look at the velocity at an instant we obtain v = 0/0, which is meaningless (Vlastos, G., "A note on Zeno's arrow", *Phronesis*, vol. 11, 1966, pp. 3–18).

4 Kandinski, Eisenman, Evans, and Lynn, among others, have experimented and articulated the concept of kinetic form and its architectural value. See Segrest, R., "The Perimeter Projects", *Perspecta* vol. 23, 1987, p. 61; Eisenman, P., "*Eisenman Studios at GSD: 1983–85*", Cambridge, MA: Harvard University Graduate School of Design, 1986; Evans, R. "Not to be used for wrapping purposes", *AA Files*, 10/85, 1985, pp. 68–74; Lynn, G., *Animate Form*, New York: Princeton Architectural Press, 1999.

5 Segrest, R., "The Perimeter Projects", *Perspecta*, vol. 23, 1987, p. 61.

6 One of the first theorists to identify and explore the idea of soft objects in architectural design is Marcos Novak. In his paper "Computational Compositions" *Computing in Design Computation, ACADIA 1988* Proceedings, ed. P.J. Bancroft, Marcos identified the three important principles of digital architecture: (a) the replacement of the finite object by the variable object, (b) the idea of pluralism replacing singularity, and (c) the existence of equally accessible information. In his work, he explores the idea of architecture as process rather than output.

Chapter 4

(Un)folding Form[1]

Folding is the process of laying one part over another. While the outcome of folding may appear as a replication of shapes, theoretically, folding is a self-referential process: no elements are added or subtracted from the folding scene. The same form inverts, reverts, and entangles in multiple ways revealing repetitive patterns. Folding is an intricate process that addresses one of form's most existential qualities: the cross from one dimension into another. It is a process that involves changes that extend the geometrical properties of an object while preserving its topology. A piece of aluminum foil, for instance, when crumpled to form a ball-like shape, embodies the properties of a three-dimensional solid object despite the fact that it is a two-dimensional surface. Similarly, a thread may be crumbled into a hairball, thus extending its properties by two dimensions.

This hidden trans-dimensional property of the folding process has a high value in nature. Proteins fold and intertwine to connect and build larger structures. Snakes and fishes fold and unfold to slide. Almost any motion the human body performs is based on folding and unfolding. From eyelids and knees to fingers and jaws, human motion is almost exclusively based on folding and unfolding limbs. Even the most elaborate movements are essentially based on intricate collaborations of folding limbs. Animal evolution is often portrayed by a creature, such as a fish, growing legs and moving out of water to start erecting in posture as it grows more elaborate limbs that eventually allow it to stand up, differentiating the role between feet and hands. This morphogenetic paradigm of evolution reveals, to a certain extent, the association of limbs with movements. The length, location, and interconnection between folding limbs allow more useful, suitable, and desirable motions. For instance the thumb, as a folding element, is grown at a certain location

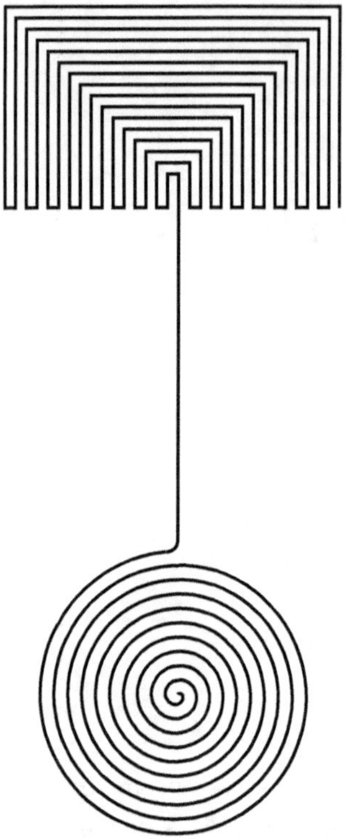

4.1
Ariadue's thread: A thread can be folded and bent in such a way as to create a two-dimensional composition

off the palm to allow certain elaborate folding motions that result in better handling, touching, rotating, and feeling.

In contrast, mechanical movement is primarily based on the invention of the wheel, an artificial creation that does not exist *per se* in nature. While a circle may also be viewed as a folded line bent to meet at each end, its Euclidean ontology points instead to the notion of "equal distance from a pivot reference".[1] The notion of equality negates the existence of two points labeled as "start" and "end" to be regarded as special. Consequently, "start" and "end" collapse into an end-less (or start-less) infinitely repetitive scheme that maps to the infinitely repetitive notion of movement. In contrast, organic matter is structured around the notion of cellular growth, which implies the existence of a "starting" point, an "ending" point, and a direction. It is because of the asymmetrical layouts of tissues, and the contractions and expansions of muscles that produce folding and unfolding schemes that eventually result in movement.

Topologically, folding is a continuous transformation, yet its inverse function, "unfolding", is not.[2] Thus, if a point P is near a subset S of the plane, after folding the point remains still near to S. In contrast, after unfolding, the point P is set far away from at least half the subset; the other half of S remains on the other side of the plane. This topological property can be associated with motion. Specifically, as the notion of "near" succeeds that of "far away", the measures of

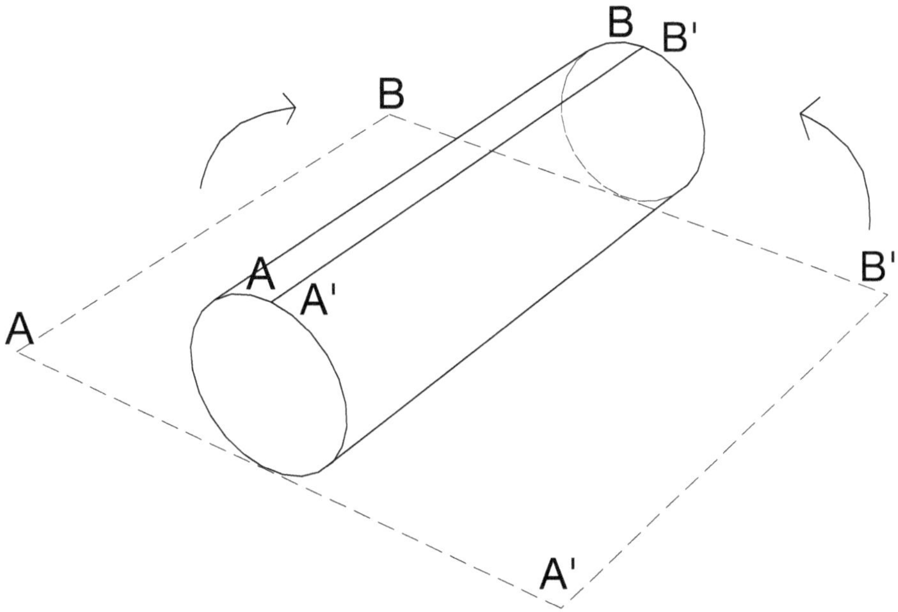

4.2
A planar surface bent into a cylinder

distance, position, and change, which are the defining constituent elements of motion, are introduced. Movement is thus accomplished not through infinite succession but rather as a result of the interchange of two opposing functions.

Folding is a term that differs from, but is often confused with, mirroring. While mirroring involves the mutual interchange of two positions, folding involves selective and exclusive mappings; it suggests directionality, partitioning, seclusion, and isolation. In Greek the word "fold" is *diploma*, which is derived from the root of double or twofold. In that sense, folding can be viewed as analogous to mirroring one half of a plane against a line. While the operation of mirroring, formulated as

$$m(x, y) = (-x, y),$$

involves an inversion from positive to negative value and vice versa, the operation of folding, formulated as

$$f(x, y) = (|x|, y),$$

involves the measure of absolute value, that is, the distance of a point from the origin.[3] Both operations involve the relocation of points by half the distance across a reference line, but in the case of folding the relocation is exclusive; no points can occupy the other side of the plane. Because of its non-commutative property, every folding operation can generate new schemes even if the same operators are involved repeatedly.

Huzita[4] formulated six axioms that map points and lines, to help construct and explain folding schemes. These axioms are based on the fact that folding is an

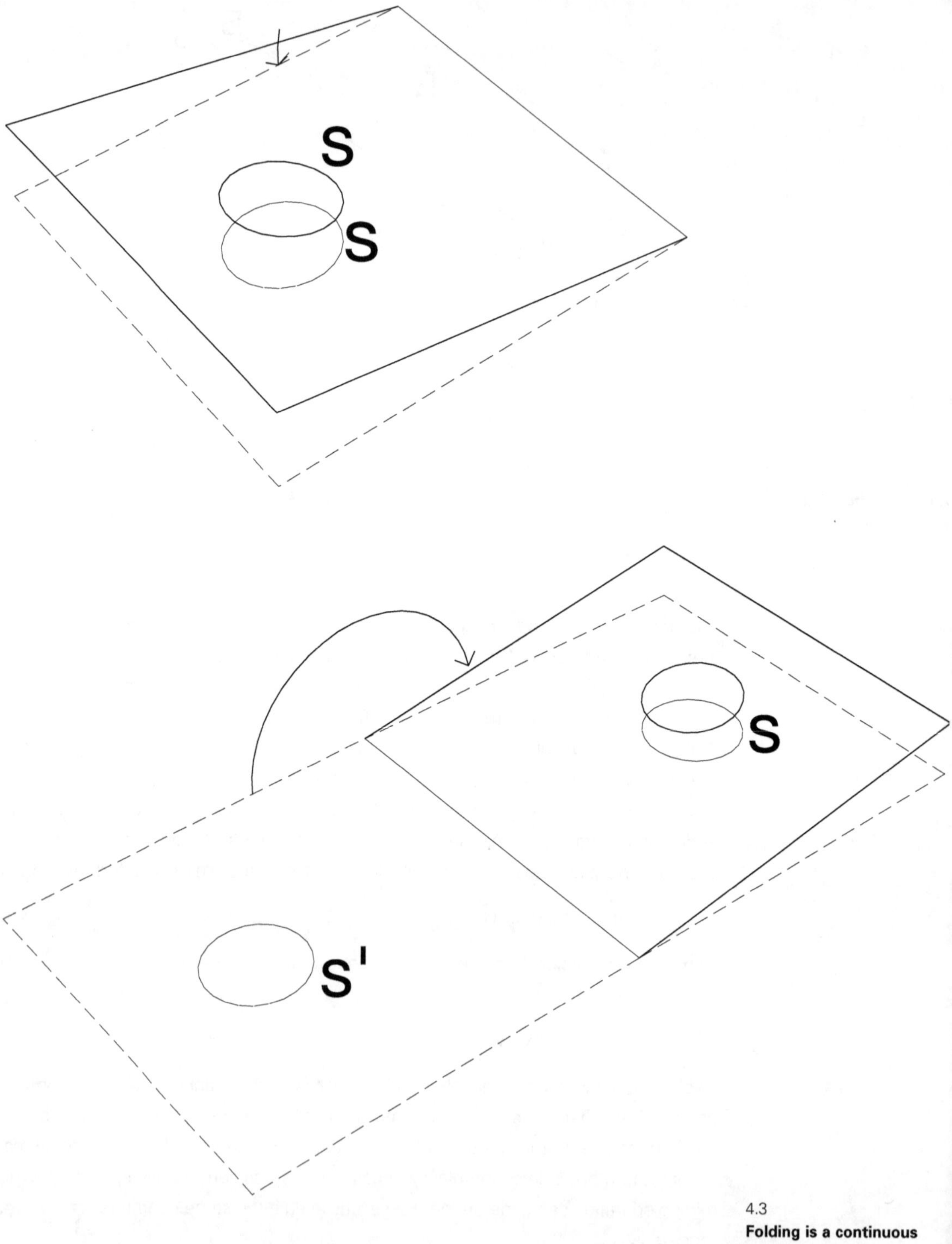

4.3
Folding is a continuous transformation, yet its inverse function, unfolding, is not

accurate, precise, and quantifiable operation. In the geometry of paper folding or origami,[5] a straight line becomes a *crease* or a *fold*. Instead of drawing straight lines, one may fold a piece of paper and flatten the crease. Although this process may appear simplistic, its value is analogous to Euclidean geometrical operations performed by using only a straight edge and a compass. Certain geometrical problems, such as trisecting an angle and doubling a cube, are impossible with these tools, yet possible with paper-folding.[6] Because of its accuracy, simplicity, and autonomy, paper-folding can contribute to the generation, analysis, and understanding of complex shapes and diagrams. Furthermore, because of its step-by-step, codifiable, rational, and modular process, paper-folding may be regarded as an algorithmic mechanism for the exploration of formal systems. In that sense, folding and unfolding become encoded processes through the logic of algorithmic computation.

Bending is a term used to denote the act of straining or moving out of a straight direction. While bending may suggest tension, stress, or restlessness, it also suggests continuity, direction, and smoothness. The notion of a bend can be associated with a differential deflection, that is, the change in direction. As a form is bending, it reaches a point where the bend transforms from a smooth deflection to a sharp crease. Even though a crease may be defined as an abrupt change in direction, the definition of "abrupt" is relative and "anexact".[7] What appears to be a sharp change may also still be regarded as a smooth transition, as we zoom in closer, as long as there is no break or tear. Continuity is the state or quality of being uninterrupted in time, sequence, substance, or extent. The notion of continuous is abstract and theoretical. While in appearance time and space appear to be continuous, it can be claimed that practically nothing is really continuous. If time and space are composed of finite elements, then there must be a disruption between two neighboring elements. In that sense, continuous transformations such as bending or folding, even though they appear to be continuous, are not.

The term "resolution" refers to the fineness of detail that can be distinguished in a discrete pattern. Practically, there is no such thing as infinite resolution. Yet from a theoretical point of view, analytic methods assume the integration of finite elements into a whole, as infinitesimally small elements form a continuous blending. This logic applies more to the senses, specifically vision, rather than the mind. Vision may be interpreted as a physiological attempt to build continuity out of discontinuity. This tendency governs the world of phenomena such that even when a threshold of invisibility is reached, it is assumed that phenomena continue to behave the same way, on and on, the same way as when they were visible. In contrast, logical consistency is a principle of human thought that may deny the existence of certain behaviors if an inconsistency occurs, regardless of the visual evidence. Continuity and discontinuity are two terms that are often conceived as opposites. In fact, deflection, inflection, bending, deviation, and disturbance are forms of discontinuity or continuity, yet none amounts to an abrupt change, break, gap, or pause. For instance, a speed bump is a disruption in the flow of traffic, yet it represents neither discontinuity nor continuity. Zeno's paradoxes dealt with the inability to demarcate the limit that separates the continuous from the discontinuous.

A finite element is a unit with finite dimensions used in a computational scheme. The notion of "finite" is often confused with physical dimensions. The demarcation of a finite element is related to the quality of uniformity within the element's domain. This delimitation is associated with a change of properties, not the area of jurisdiction. The rules for discretization of a structure into finite elements must satisfy certain requirements, such as that of common boundary and geometric approximation. The behavior of a finite element affects its neighbors and propagates throughout the structure. For instance, a shell is a structure which can be derived from a thin plate by forming it into a singly curved surface. In the theory of the finite element method, it is assumed that the behavior of a continuously curved surface can be adequately represented by the behavior of a surface built up of small, flat elements. This assumption, and its consequent scientific implementation, is an attempt to infer by inductive reasoning. Rather than assuming a continuous behavior that governs all finite elements, the behavior of each finite element contributes toward a generalized behavior. Finite elements can be regarded not as arbitrary units but rather as localized samples. In this context, general principles are derived from particular instances.

Homogeneity is the quality of being uniform in structure or composition throughout. In contrast, assemblage is the act of bringing parts together into a group or a whole. Assemblage is about composing, collecting, accumulating, congregating, and building. Homogeneity is about similarity, uniformity, and continuity. Assemblage is a process and as such involves time as a measure of progress. Because of this association with time, assemblage is regarded as a finite process. In contrast, homogeneity is about a *state*, *condition*, or *quality* of form. It is not about the action of *becoming* but rather about the accomplishment of *being*. The lack of time implies eternity, infinity, and transcendency.

Folding or bending are continuous and homogeneous transformations that preserve the integrity, continuity, and uniformity of the parts involved. It is intuitively clear that if a sheet of paper is bent into various shapes smoothly and without stretching, the resulting surfaces are all isometric and isomorphic. This property implies continuity and self-preservation, which are essential for eternal existence. Furthermore, because of its connotative association with purity, uniformity, and cleanliness, homogeneity is by extension associated with virtue, integrity, and morality. Historically, these qualities have become cultural means of expressing spirituality, divinity, and eternity. For instance, the word diploma, which in Greek means twofold, is a symbol of authenticity or certification. Similarly, heterogeneous compositions, such as temples or monuments, are built and coated to suggest homogeneity even though they may represent an assemblage of unrelated parts.

Unfolding is a term used to denote the process of opening, spreading out, or extending something folded. The prefix "un-" denotes reversal, opposition, or contrast to an action. It also assumes the existence of an action without which the reversion cannot happen. The complementary duality of these actions ensures that for every pair of reverse actions the scene returns to its initial state, as if nothing had happened. Unfolding and then folding back can happen repeatedly and yet at any moment there are only two possibilities. This obviously evident, yet redundantly important property reveals a repetitive pattern of events where time is of no importance. Instead, the focus is set to the in-between time span when folding is understood as "potentiality". For instance, a folded sheet is not understood as an isolated, independent, or complete object but rather as a hidden, latent, or virtual potentiality to deploy. Rather than approaching folding or unfolding as isolated operations, they should be understood as a complementary unified pair, the importance of which lies in between, as the one operation owes its existence to the absence (or the potential existence) of the other.

While the term unfolding may be literally understood as the reverse process of folding, the connotations associated with the notion of unfolding extend beyond simple reversion. Unfolding is also understood as a gradual revelation by written or spoken explanation. It suggests disclosure, revelation, elucidation, clarification, and explanation. In this context, the notion of unfold is understood as opposite to that of obscurity, indistinctiveness, mess, and intricacy. Consequently, unfolding can be associated with the revelation of a pattern. For instance, after unfolding a paper model until it reaches a flat configuration, a clearly defined crease pattern is formed. This pattern is the imprinted revelation of a process. Conversely, a folded model is not a composition or an assemblage but rather the encapsulation of intricate series of folding transformations.

Another geometric characteristic of crease patterns is that they display several types of symmetric organizations. The formation in 4.4(a) presents a bi-axial symmetric and repetitive organization of tiles. The formation of 4.4(b) is characterized by a rotational symmetry around a point. The pattern in 4.4(a) is invariable under *n*-mirroring processes, whereas the pattern in 4.4(b) is invariable under *n*-fold rotations about the center.

A close observation and study of the kinematics of folding structures reveals that each one of the tiles, which occur from the intersection of crease lines, performs as part of a mechanism.[8] The entire structure can be described as an assembly of moving parts. In this context it becomes obvious that any changes in the features of the crease pattern will change the relationship between the tiles, the kinematics of the structure, and the interim and final geometric configurations of the structure.

The possibility of using kinematics opens up a more intricate relationship between folding and motion than has been previously possible. Rather than conceiving of folded structures as static configurations or dynamic expressions, they may instead be conceived as transformational mechanisms. Folds and bends are not only mechanisms for structural, static, or dynamic support, but also means of kinematic exploration. It would thus seem that folding, as a moving mechanism, should be at odds with its homogeneous timeless nature. And yet this is not so, in

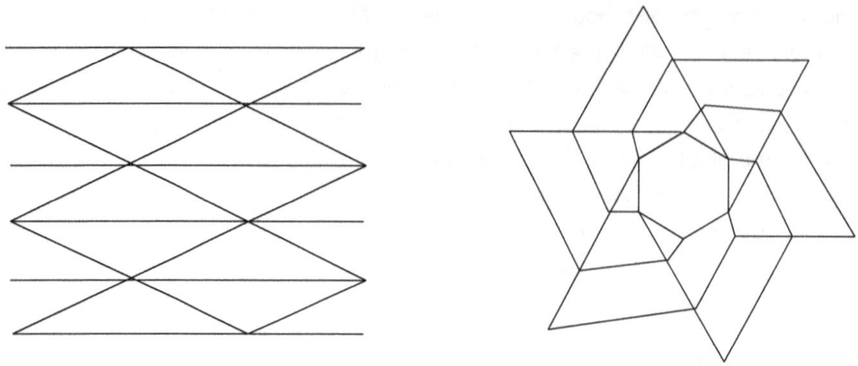

(a) (b)

4.4
Origami crease patterns

at least two ways. First, homogeneity is not only a quality of form or matter; its association with uniformity and continuity can be extended to address time-based continuous or synchronous events. Second, timelessness is a notion based not only on the absence of time, but also on the notion of infinity; repetitive events, reoccurring moments, and iterative episodes, when they take place at equal time spans, suggest a circular time effect where start and end collapse into an infinite continuum.

In this context, an observation of the kinematics of different foldable structures also shows a variety of factors that may affect the behavior of folding and unfolding structures: symmetry, synchronicity, and sequence to name but a few. For instance, in a symmetrical asynchronous sequential configuration distinct steps follow a propagation effect, whereas in a synchronously deploying structure all tiles move at the same time and the motion of one affects the motion of all other tiles adjacent to it.

The dominant mode for discussing the notion of folding in architecture has been that of an aesthetics paradigm. Beginning with Deleuze's work *The Fold: Leibniz and the Baroque*,[9] in which he draws parallels between the philosophy of Leibniz and the expressionism of the Baroque movement, his statement that "the smallest element of the labyrinth is the fold, not the point"[10] may be interpreted as a basis for the rejection of Cartesian geometry in favor of neutral and singular architectural systems. Since then, terms such as pliancy, smoothness, and striated are used extensively within the architectural discourse that accompanies the movement.

A few architectural designers and theorists, Greg Lynn being the most lucid among them, argue for the ability to integrate unrelated elements within a new continuous mixture through folding. Folding became the method by which homogeneity could be differentiated while remaining continuous. According to Lynn, "pliancy allows architecture to become involved in complexity through flexibility."[11] In a way, his position is a compromise between two opposite cultural and formal contexts: conflict and contradiction versus unity and reconstruction.

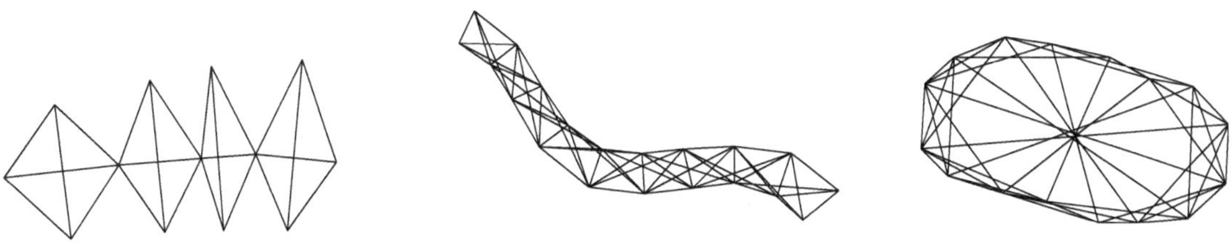

4.5
Masses, springs and muscles working together

Similarly, Eisenmann defines folds, bends, and cusps as points of change caused by events intrinsic to the form itself. This position leads him to depart from Cartesian geometry as an observer's world and move the discourse to address topological qualities of the form itself. From that point of view, fold becomes a means for achieving dynamism not as a temporal quality but rather as a potentiality, or as a becoming. In the schematic drawings for the Alteca office building in Tokyo, a series of dual operations, such as folding/unfolding, envolve/involve, or contract/dilate are used to explore the relationship between fold and time. The final form can be described as an emerging yet disappearing, deploying yet retracting, folding yet unfolding event.

The problem with these approaches is that they assume the existence of a human-conceived global scheme that governs all formal events. According to these approaches, form is assumed to be an abstract entity shaped by forces that "are capable of complex deformations in response to programmatic, structural, economic, aesthetic, political, and contextual influences".[12] This premise results from a logic which tends to explain phenomena by inferring from the general to the specific. By doing so it accomplishes universality, conformity, and consistency, which are principles that the human mind abides by. Regardless of the methods or techniques used to form a principle, once it is formed it becomes a shaping force that permits it to interpret, explain, and predict structures and behaviors. For instance, in the work of biologist Thompson, a system of geometric coordinates was used to inscribe the outline of an organism.[13] He was then able to obtain the figures of other species under homogeneous strains of the coordinate system. Essentially, what Thompson was doing was to use a human-conceived global scheme (geometry) to interpret, explain, and predict structures and connections of a cellular formal event (organic growth). While universality as a scope or range of knowledge may be a virtue of human thought, it certainly cannot be applied to everything.

In contrast, through inductive reasoning, general principles are derived from particular facts or instances. While this approach may be regarded as weak due to lack of adequate statistical samples or sufficient combinatorial processing, yet, in our present age, computational methods allow such reasoning to exhibit robust, complete, and verifiable characteristics. Because of new advancements in database management and computability, concepts or procedures once regarded as complex are increasingly reduced to simple tasks. Thus, the emphasis has shifted away from a search for global principles to explain local phenomena and towards the study of local principles to explain global phenomena. For instance, finite element methods have been used extensively to explore deformations of forms under stress as an alternative to analytical methods, which are based on general principles of physics. The difference is that finite element methods incorporate a degree of unpredictability due to their computational nature. In that sense, they negate complete control to the human mind and as such are not verifiable through human-based common sense. The result of complex calculations, based on finite element methods, are far more accurate, often revealing behaviors that amaze even the programmers or scientists who devised those methods. In contrast, formal experiments using human-based principles may display interesting relationships but are certainly not unpredictable.

The use, therefore, of computers to experiment with human-based philosophical systems is a contradictory logic. How much more – other than rendering – can a computer contribute to a philosophical scheme that is already preconceived in one person's mind? At the same time, how much can a computer contribute to a philosophical argument when it has no criticality built into it?

Rather than investing in arrested conflicts, a cooperation of both approaches may lead to synergies between opposite, yet complementary, intellects in the pursuit of truth, discovery, or exploration: the human mind with its ability to abstract, generalize, and deduce and the "digital mind" with its ability to compute, combine, and induce. Limitations or weaknesses can be transformed into extensions or strengths. Neither position should stand on its own, but both should benefit from the other. Rather than drawing lines of conflict, philosophical terms might be better exploited by computational methods. For the first time perhaps, the human intellect might be aligned with neither skepticism nor tautology but with rebirth and transformation.

Challenging these conflicts, architecture finds itself in the middle of theoretical discourse and practical implementation. More than ever now, through the use of simulated design spaces and microelectronic controllers, actual motion can be designed, tested, and implemented in real or virtual buildings. The traditional problematic of enclosure, form, and order are inflected and transformed by the new spatial possibilities and strategies opened up through technological intervention, particularly digital technologies and a new spatial relationship to information. The concept of responsive environments – the integration of intelligent computers, sensors, and actuators into the built environment – and the impact such results has upon the designs of buildings are of paramount importance to the field of architecture. While the aesthetic value of folding may always be a source of inspiration, its kinematic implementation may challenge the very nature of what architecture really is.

Notes

1 According to Edmund Husserl, "geometry arises when the factual limits of measurement and dealing with anexact morphology is surpassed toward an ideal limit of infinite exactitude, when roundness is replaced by the circle". See Deridda, J., *Edmund Husserl's Origin of Geometry: An Introduction*, trans. J. Leavey, Portland, OR: Book News, 1978, p. 127.

2 See Janich, K., *Topology*, UTM, New York: Springer-Verlag, 1984.

3 *Reflection* in y-axis f: D((a,b),r)->D((-a,b),r), where f(x,y) = (-x,y) is continuous and topological. *Folding* f: R^2->R^{2+}, where R^{2+} is the right half-plane and f(x,y) = (|x|,y) is continuous but not topological.

4 The Italian–Japanese mathematician Humiaki Huzita has formulated a powerful set of paper-folding axioms (see Huzita, H., "Understanding Geometry through Origami Axioms" in *Proceedings of the First International Conference on Origami in Education and Therapy* (COET91), ed. J. Smith, London: British Origami Society, 1992, pp. 37–70):

1 Given two points *p1* and *p2* we can fold a line connecting them.
2 Given two points *p1* and *p2* we can fold *p1* onto *p2*.
3 Given two lines *l1* and *l2* we can fold line *l1* onto *l2*.
4 Given a point *p1* and a line *l1* we can make a fold perpendicular to *l1* passing through the point *p1*.
5 Given two points *p1* and *p2* and a line *l1* we can make a fold that places *p1* onto *l1* and passes through the point *p2*.
6 Given two points *p1* and *p2* and two lines *l1* and *l2* we can make a fold that places *p1* onto line *l1* and places *p2* onto line *l2*.

5 Origami is the art of paper-folding. The word is Japanese, literally meaning to fold (*oru*) paper (*kami*).

6 See Huzita, H., "The trisection of a given angle solved by the geometry of origami", *Proceedings of the First International Meeting of Origami Science and Technology*, H. Huzita, Pomona, CA: 1989, pp. 195–214.

7 "Anexact" as Deleuze and Guattari put it are "zones of indeterminacy" whose topology is inconsistent, whose contours are vague. But this indeterminacy is not a subjective illusion, not the result of insufficient precision. Rather, it is a perfectly objective indeterminacy: an effect that is well defined in its own right.

8 See Liapi, K, "Transformable Architecture Inspired by the Origami Art: Computer Visualization as a Tool for Form Exploration", *ACADIA Proceedings*, ed. G. Procter, Pomona: CA, 2002: Claifornia Polytechnic at Pomona: pp. 385–392.

9 See Deleuze, G., *The Fold: Leibniz and the Baroque*, Trans. T. Conley, Minneapolis: University of Minnesota Press, 1993.

10 Ibid., p. 6.

11 See Lynn, G., "Architectural Curvilinearity", in *Architecture and Science*, G. Di Cristina ed. London: AD Press, 2001, p. 26. (An earlier version of that paper is in Lynn, G., "Architectural Curvilinearity: The Folded, The Pliant and the Supple," in *Folding in Architecture*, ed. G. Lynn, AD Profile 102, London: Academy Editions, 1993, p. 8.)

12 Di Cristina, Ibid., 27.

13 See Thompson, D., *On Growth and Form*, Cambridge: Cambridge University Press, 1961, p. 272.

Chapter 5

Warped Eye

Perspective systems are designed to construct pictures that, when viewed, produce in the trained viewer the experience of depicted objects that match perceivable objects. Space perception theorists[1] have written about how our capacities to see are constrained by the perspective system that we use, that is, by our way of depicting what we see. In the arts, the methods of depiction are of significant importance as they are the means of expression and description of imaginary worlds. Artists and designers engage in storytelling and offer a glimpse into their fantasy worlds through unique, personal, private, and idiosyncratic visual methods.

Pictorial spaces are constructed through geometrical models. Each model is expressed as a geometrical transformation applied to Cartesian shapes of the physical environment. These transformations show how shapes are projected in pictorial space. For instance, the mapping of a cube residing in Cartesian space is projected to the surface of the viewing plane through straight lines representing light rays.

In architecture, the methods of projection also serve a subliminal purpose. While axonometric views are considered exact, precise, accurate, and measurable, perspective views are empirical, observable, factual, and expressive. Perspective projection is about the viewer's identity, existence, location, and orientation, while orthographic projection is about the depicted object's identity and characteristics. Isometric and oblique views are exaggerated and, often, extreme methods of orthographic projection whose purpose is to express, focus, and attract attention to certain parts or angles of the depicted form. Another model of depiction is that of abstraction: black-and-white line drawings convey a clear, sharp, and sterile impression of the depicted form, whereas blueprints are understood as working drawings. In

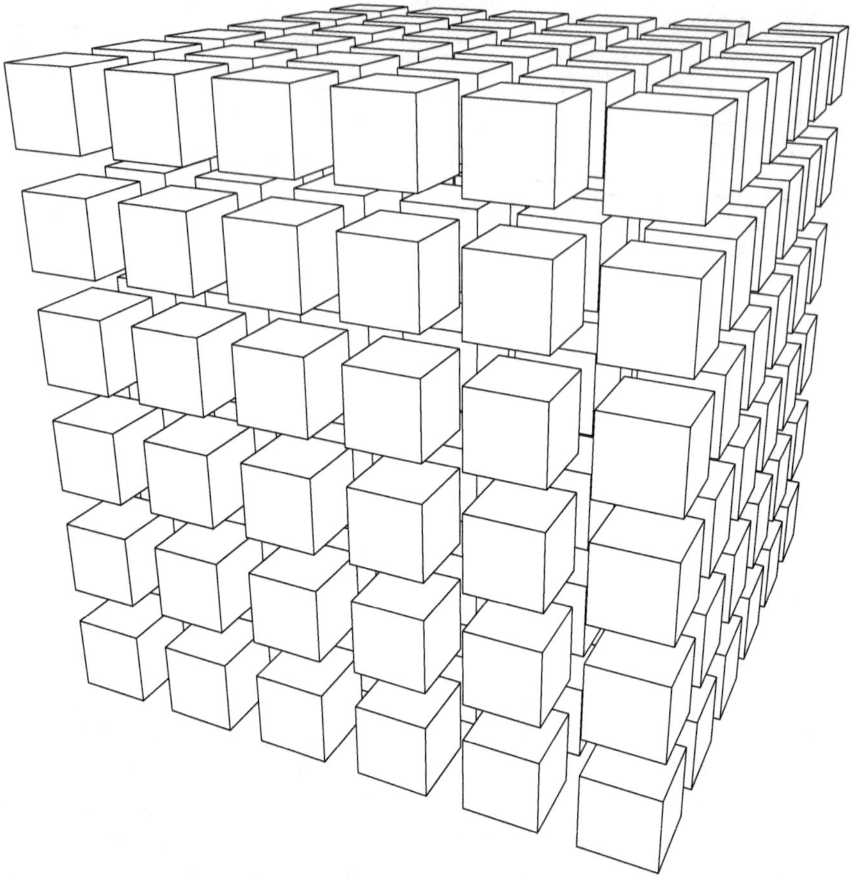

5.1
Perspective projection

contrast, rendered drawings convey materiality, completeness, substance, and effect. The problem with rendered views is that form is not always conceived as made out of matter. In fact, form is rather an abstract entity that possesses certain geometric characteristics. For instance, dots on a piece of paper may imply a shape not because they are made out of ink but because of their geometric relationships. The attachment of material qualities constrains the behavior of form and restricts the designer's imagination. In contrast, the lack of materiality liberates the form from its constraints and introduces behaviors closer to intuition rather than perception.

Often reality is considered as the ultimate objective for the representation of architectural scenes.[2] While the computer-graphical search for an indistinguishable representation of reality is, in essence, a search for completeness, its value as a means of architectural communication is debatable. Reality is about actuality, perfection, completeness, and objectivity. Nonetheless, the notions of incompleteness, imperfection, and subjectivity have a complementary value that often surpasses that of an explicit presentation. Tacit, suggestive, connotative, implicit, subtle, and evocative are qualities that invite the viewer to participate in the visual composition.

5.2
Inverted perspective projection

Sketching, drawing, or painting are means of visual expression aimed not at representing reality as it is, but rather in implying, suggesting, and inviting the viewer to explore and participate in how reality may be.

Consistency is a phenomenon that ties together seemingly disparate entities. Traditionally, projection systems were constructed to simulate reality, either subjective or objective, using the principles of optics. In that context, movement in a simulated three-dimensional space under the rules of perspective projection should be consistent with one's own experience of physical movement. Any distortion to the rules of optics should, in turn, distort the simulated environment.[3] The distortion may not be recognized by reference to previous experience, but it is consistent within the new rules. More than ever now, through the use of applied physics and computation, design space can become a dynamic simulation environment for the exploration of visual behaviors far beyond experience or prediction.

The work of Gauss, Riemann, von Helmholtz, and Clifford[4] showed that geometries could be based on relationships other than Euclidean. This altered the notion of geometry by revealing its abstract postulational character and removed it from any connection to the structure of empirical intuition. Spaces can be constructed on the basis of non-Euclidean axioms revealing behaviors closer to our sensations rather than our perception. For example, if we assume that visual space is hyperbolic and physical space is Cartesian, it is possible to derive a comparative model of mapping between the two spaces, allowing a totally different conceptualization of space. Such a model is expressed as a hyperbolic transformation applied to Euclidean/Cartesian shapes of the physical environment. The result is a hallucinating view of pictorial space where every form in the scene *appears* to be a caricature.[5] Luneburg's[6] idea of hyperbolic space was a first attempt to develop a theory of visual space in which geometrical structure is a metric space of constant, probably negative, Gaussian curvature.

More than ever now through the use of computer tools and visualization techniques, art and architecture find themselves in a position to rediscover and challenge their traditional methods of depiction. Designers are presented with tools that allow them to manipulate the overall order, organization, and representation of their forms, thus replacing a single design with a range of designs. The new soft and workable design space negates the singularity of the old rigid space and asserts the freedom of an open system where change is celebrated.[7] New emphasis is placed

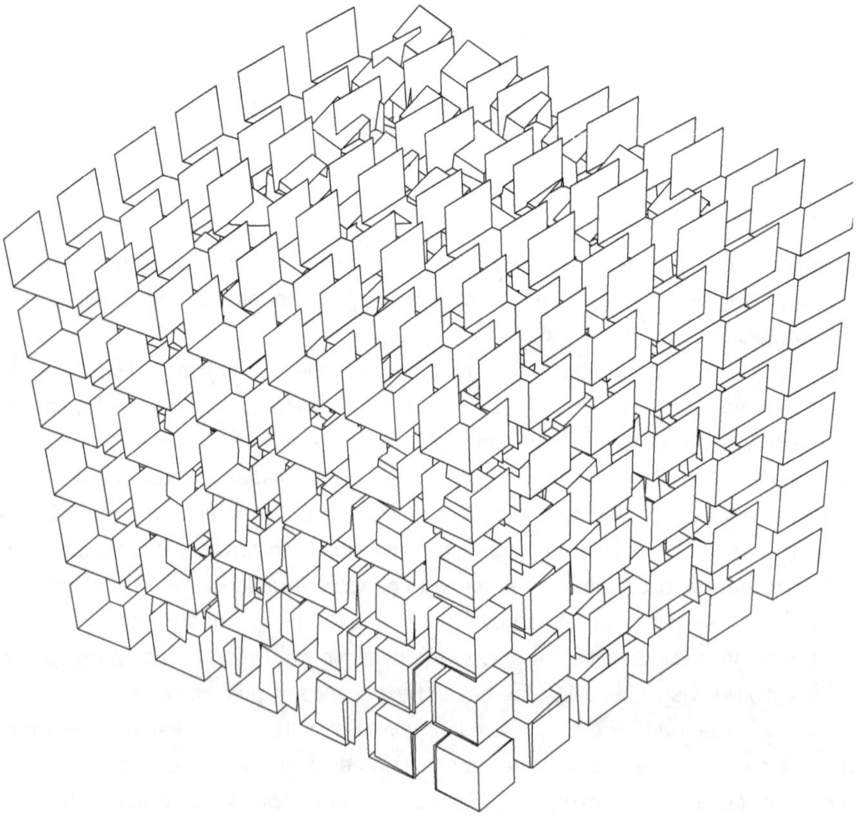

5.3
Multi-viewer projection; each face of each object in the scene is projected along a different point of view. Specifically, different projection methods are used to depict every other face of each object along different values of the viewing distance *d*, that is, either *d* or −*d*. From the viewer's point of view, faces of objects seem to move in opposite directions at the same time as the scene is rotated

$face_{2n} \rightarrow view_{-d}$
$face_{2n+1} \rightarrow view_{d}$

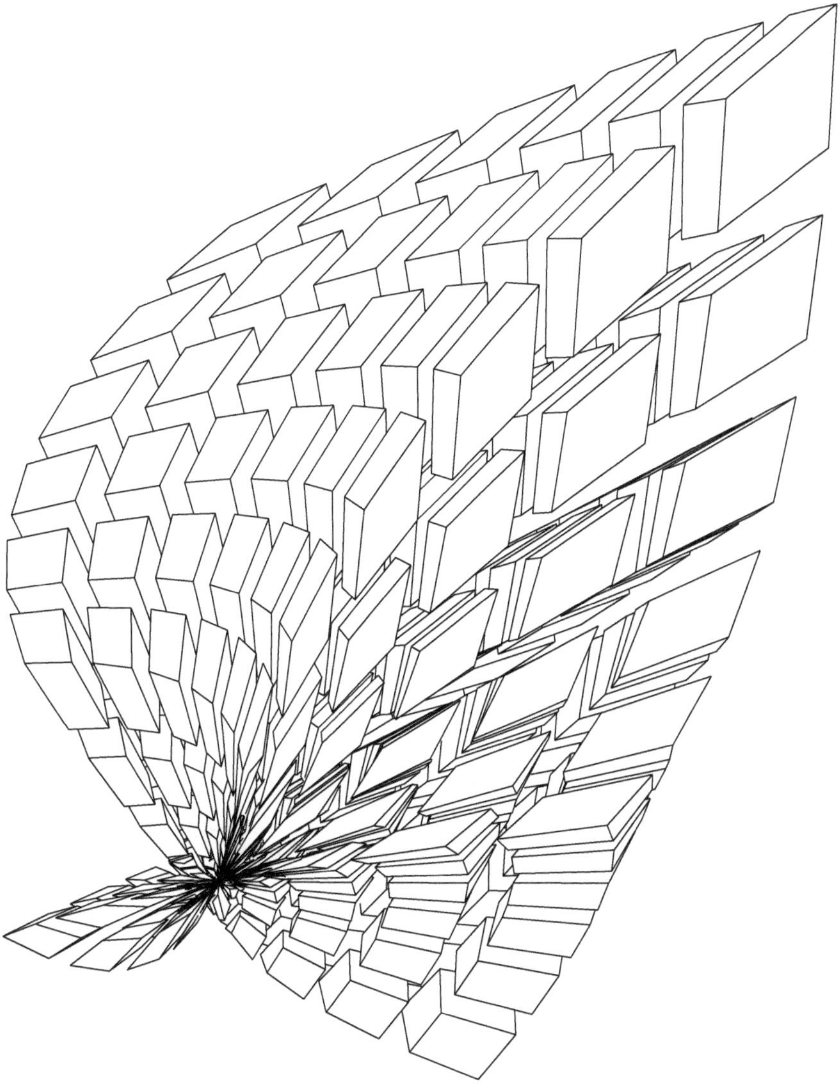

5.4
Projection of a point (*x, y, z*) on a viewing plane does not have to occur along a straight line

on curvature and proportion and therefore on organic and dynamic relations. The surprise of the unexpected result infuses new energy to the act of conceiving as well as experiencing form.

In response to architecture's struggle to critically embrace and understand the new possibilities, two approaches have been dominant; either a reevaluation of past theories and practices in search for parallel or reoccurring themes or a search for new unprecedented themes that owe their existence to concepts and mechanisms foreign, alien, or external to the discipline of architecture.

The first approach builds upon historical precedence and seeks to metaphorically or indirectly associate past concepts with new ones, ultimately aiming

5.5
Hyperbolic projection mapping

at establishing a historical continuity and evolution. For instance, Lynn attempts to relate philosophical, mathematical, or biological theories to explain and justify computational phenomena. He states "just as the development of calculus drew upon the historical mathematical developments that preceded it, so too will an animate approach to architecture subsume traditional models of statics into a more advanced system of dynamic organizations".[8] Similarly, Vidler looks into new digital techniques while relying on traditional perspectives. He states "the notion of an architecture developed out of topologies rather than typologies nevertheless introduces a fundamental rupture into theory if not into practice".[9]

In contrast, the second approach builds toward a new theoretical framework necessary to critically evaluate computational phenomena by seeking evidence beyond previous understanding or outside the context of architecture. For instance, Novak extends the notion of virtuality beyond light, shadow or sampling and introduces the notions of inversion, immersion, and eversion. Essentially, he seeks changes in the quest for knowledge since "definitions, disciplines, institutions have all become unstable and inadequate, and everywhere there are reevaluations of the structures by which we comprehend the world".[10] Similarly, Lonsway detects incompleteness in the digital representation of space and time, and inquires into extending the literal coordinate dimensions into a realm where an "*n*-dimensional framework" captures the essence of computational space.[11]

A challenging point is the fact that this new aesthetics is about the unknown, the unpredictable, and the unforeseeable. It requires the cooperation of two brains: that of the human and the computer, for without one another it is impossible to plan or execute imaginary design spaces. Most of all, they lead to the creation of computational schemes, which are available for experimentation, analysis or play across disciplines. Dynamic design space contributes to our understanding of aesthetics and creates a new dimension of how it may change our perception. It also brings up a social point: who is the creator? How will it change our perception if science and mathematics can mold into the creative process?

Notes

1 Panofsky, E., *Perspective as Symbolic Form*, trans. C. S. Wood, Cambridge, MA: MIT Press, 1997.

2 One of the long-term goals of computer graphics has been the reproduction of realistic scenes. See, for instance, Tole, P., Pellacini, F., Walter, B. and Greenberg, D. "Interactive Global Illumination in Dynamic Scenes", in *SIGGRAPH 2002 Conference Proceedings*, John F. Hughes, ed. New York: ACM Press, ACM SIGGRAPH, July 2002, pp. 537–546.

3 In the paintings of Giorgio De Chirico, multiple perspective systems within the same scene create a feeling of insecurity and uneasiness. For instance, in *Nostalgia dell' infinito* (1913) the tower, the building, and the box all have different vanishing points, none of which meets at the horizon.

4 Clifford, W. K., *The Common Sense of Exact Sciences*, New York: Knopf, 1946. First published in 1885.

5 Heelan, P. offers an extensive survey on *Space-perception and the Philosophy of Science*, Berkeley: University of California Press, 1988. Also Lunenburg, R. in his paper "The Metric of Visual Space", *Journal of the Optical Society of America*, vol. 40, 1950, pp. 627–642 offers a description of hyperbolic space. A simulation of the mapping between physical and visual space has been implemented as a real-time computational application in Terzidis, K., "Experiments on Projection Systems", *ACADIA Quarterly*, vol. 16, no. 4, 1999, pp. 8–15.

6 Lunenburg, R. ibid.

7 One of the first theorists to identify and explore the idea of soft objects in architectural design was Marcos Novak. In his paper "Computational Compositions" (*ACADIA 1988 Proceedings*) Marcos identified the three important principles of digital architecture: (a) the replacement of the finite object by the variable object, (b) the idea of pluralism replacing singularity, and (c) the existence of equally accessible information. In his work, he explores the idea of architecture as process rather than output.

8 See Lynn, G., *Animate Form*, New York: Princeton Architectural Press, 1999, p. 9.

9 See Vidler, A., *Warped Spaces*, Cambridge, MA: MIT Press, 2001, p. 227.

10 According to Novak "we can distinguish five degrees of virtuality, as related to screens and hypersurfaces: *light and shadow:* projections of absence and presence: mirrors, shadow theatres, Plato's Cave; *sampling and statistics:* constructions of continuity from discontinuity, connotation from denotation: zoetropes, cinema, television, digital sound, transitions from discrete to continuous space and back by processes of digital-to-analogue and analogue-to-digital conversions; *inversion:* computation and epistemology, seeing through knowing, scientific visualisation, simulations, computer graphics, special effects; *immersion:* alteration, cyberspace, virtual reality, casting the world into the virtual;

eversion: casting the virtual unto the world, multi-threading virtual/real and actual/possible." See Novak M., "Transarchitectures and Hypersurfaces", in *Architecture and Science*, G. Di Cristina, ed. London: AD Press, 2001, pp. 153–157.

11 See Lonsway, B., "The Mistaken Dimensionality of CAD", *Journal of Architectural Education*, vol. 56 no. 2, November 2002, pp. 22–25.

Chapter 6

Algorithmic Form

An algorithm is a computational procedure for addressing a problem in a finite number of steps. It involves deduction, induction, abstraction, generalization, and structured logic. It is the systematic extraction of logical principles and the development of a generic solution plan. Algorithmic strategies utilize the search for repetitive patterns, universal principles, interchangeable modules, and inductive links. The intellectual power of an algorithm lies in its ability to infer new knowledge and to extend certain limits of the human intellect.

While many algorithms have been invented and implemented for architectural design in space allocation and planning problems,[1] their implementation in aesthetics and formal theories has been, generally, limited. Most of the theories related to form pertain mainly to subjective interpretation and perception. In contrast, algorithmic logic involves a deterministic approach to form and its shaping forces; it suggests rationality, consistency, coherency, organization, and systemization. What makes algorithmic logic so problematic for architects is that they have maintained an ethos of artistic sensibility and intuitive playfulness in their practice. In contrast, because of its mechanistic nature, an algorithm is perceived as a non-human creation and therefore is considered distant and remote. Traditionally, the dominant mode for discussing creativity in architecture has always been that of intuition and talent, where stylistic ideas are pervaded by an individual, a "star," or a group of talented partners within the practice. In contrast, an algorithm is a procedure, the result of which is not necessarily credited to its creator. Algorithms are understood as abstract and universal mathematical operations that can be applied to almost any kind or any quantity of elements. For instance, an algorithm in computational geometry is not about the person who invented it but rather about its efficiency, speed, and generality.

Consequently, the use of algorithms to address formal problems is regarded suspiciously by some[2] as an attempt to overlook human sensitivity and creativity and give credit instead to an anonymous, mechanistic, and automated procedure.[3]

While most algorithms are tailored to automate tedious manual methods, there is a certain category of algorithms that are not aimed at predictable results. Their inductive strategy is to explore generative processes or to simulate complex phenomena. Such inductive algorithms can be regarded as extensions to human thinking and therefore may allow one to leap into areas of unpredictable, unimaginable, and often inconceivable potential. For instance, artificial neural networks are systems of algorithms that simulate the human brain's functions. They are being used in classification, forecasting, and modeling applications. In making determinations, neural networks use several principles, including gradient-based training, fuzzy logic, genetic algorithms, and Bayesian methods. What distinguishes these algorithmic processes from common algorithms is that their behavior is often non-predictable and that frequently they produce patterns of thought and results that amaze even their own creators. Similarly in design, shape grammars, mathematical models, topological properties, genetic systems, mappings, and morphisms are algorithmic processes aimed at exploring uncommon, unpredictable, and uncharted formal properties and behaviors.[4]

Two opposing human activities that are central to algorithmic composition as a mode of thought are invention and discovery. Invention is defined as the act of causing something to exist by the use of ingenuity or imagination; it is an artificial human creation. In contrast, discovery is the act of encountering, for the first time, something that already existed. Both invention and discovery are about the origin of ideas and their existence in the context of human understanding. These two intellectual mechanisms result from a logic which tends to argue whether the existence of certain ideas or processes is one of the following: either a human creation or simply a glimpse of an already existing universe regardless of the presence of humans. The most paradigmatic example of this polemic is that of geometry itself: the existence of geometry can be regarded as either a descriptive revelation of properties, measurements, and relationships of existing forms or as an arbitrary, postulate-based mental structure that exists only in the human mind. For instance, Euclidean geometry was developed originally to measure distances on the surface of earth and yet, in Euclidean geometry, Platonic primitive shapes, such as squares, circles, and triangles, do not exist *per se* in nature though they represent idealized approximations of natural objects. Likewise, architecture can be regarded as either a simulation of the laws and structure of nature or as a world of fantasy and imagination.[5] In any case, algorithms are encapsulations of processes or systems of processes that allow one to leap and venture into the world of the unknown, whether natural or artificial. They are not the end product, but rather a vehicle for exploration.

Computation is a term that differs from, but is often confused with, computerization. While computation is the procedure of calculating, i.e., determining something by mathematical or logical methods, computerization is the act of entering, processing, or storing information in a computer or a computer system.[6] Computerization is about automation, mechanization, digitization, and conversion. Generally, it involves the digitization of entities or processes that are preconceived, predetermined, and well defined. In contrast, computation is about the exploration of indeterminate, vague, unclear, and often ill-defined processes; because of its exploratory nature, computation aims at emulating or extending the human intellect. It is about rationalization, reasoning, logic, algorithm, deduction, induction, extrapolation, exploration and estimation. In its manifold implications, it involves problem solving, mental structures, cognition, simulation, and rule-based intelligence, to name but a few.

Digitization is the conversion of analog information into digital information. Computerization, by definition, involves digitization. This is not necessarily the case with computation. Because many mental processes can be analyzed, codified, systematized or even synthesized without the use of computers, computational methods do not have to involve digitization. Nonetheless, their implementation on a computer system allows explorations of complexities that extend the limits of human prediction. For instance, even though the work of Gaston Julia[7] in the 1920s and, consequently, Benoit Mandelbrot[8] in the 1970s were conceived and expressed in paper, they would have never been visualized, understood, and explored further without the use of computational graphics.

Computing is a term used to denote the *act* of making a mathematical calculation or a computation. Computing is often equated with computation since both employ the same methods. Essentially, both terms share the same meaning. Grammatically, the term computation involves the suffix "-tion" that denotes a *state*, *condition*, or *quality* of a procedure. Similarly, the term computing employs the suffix "-ing" that implies an *action* of implementing a procedure. While the two terms are linked through a state–action relationship, the noun "computation" implies a set of theories and methods, whereas the noun "computing" suggests an active investigation within the sphere of computation. In any case, these two terms are entirely different, distinguished, and set apart from the terms computerization or digitization.

The dominant mode of utilizing computers in architecture today is that of computerization; entities or processes that are already conceptualized in the designer's mind are entered, manipulated, or stored in a computer system. In contrast, computation or computing, as a computer-based design tool, is generally limited. The problem with this situation is that designers do not take advantage of the computational power of the computer. Instead some venture into manipulations or criticisms of computer models as if they were products of computation. While research and development of software involves extensive computational techniques, mouse-based manipulations of three-dimensional computer models are not necessarily acts of computation. For instance, it appears, from the current discourse, that mouse-based manipulations of control points on non-uniform rational b-spline (NURBS)-based surfaces are considered by some theorists to be acts of computing.[9] While the mathematical concept and software implementation of NURBS as surfaces is a product of applied numerical computation, the rearrangement of their control points through commercial software is simply an affine transformation, i.e. a translation.

An alternative choice is being formulated that may escape these dialectically opposed strategies: algorithmic design. It involves the designation of software programs to generate space and form from the rule-based logic inherent in architectural programs, typologies, building code, and language itself. Instead of direct programming, the codification of design intention using scripting languages available in three-dimensional packages (i.e. Maya Embedded Language (MEL), 3dMaxScript, and FormZ) can build consistency, structure, coherency, traceability, and intelligence into computerized three-dimensional form. By using scripting languages designers can go beyond the mouse, transcending the factory-set limitations of current three-dimensional software. Algorithmic design does not eradicate differences but incorporates both computational complexity and creative use of computers. For architects, algorithmic design enables the role of the designer to shift from architecture programming to programming architecture. Rather than investing in arrested conflicts, computational terms might be better exploited by this alternative choice. For the first time perhaps, architectural design might be aligned with neither formalism nor rationalism but with intelligent form and traceable creativity.

There are still some misconceptions about the role of the computer in the process of design. Design, like many other mental processes, at the information-processing level has nothing specifically neural about it. The functional equivalence between brains and computers does not imply any structural equivalence at an anatomical level (e.g., equivalence of neurons with circuits). Theories of information processes are not equivalent to theories of neural or electronic mechanisms for information processing.[10] Even though, physically, computers may appear to be a set of mindless connections, at the information level they are the materialization of mathematical and syllogistic procedures.[11]

The word "tool" is often used to describe the synergistic interaction of designers with computers. A tool is defined as an instrument used in the performance of an operation. The connotative notion of a tool implies control, power, dominance, skill, and artistry. A pen, for instance, is a device that allows one to perform or facilitate the manual or mechanical work of writing or drawing. The capabilities, potency, and limitations of a tool are known or estimated in advanced. This is not the case with computers performing inductive algorithmic computations. Neither is their capacity or potency understood, nor can their limitations be pre-estimated. Indeed, designers are frequently amazed by processes performed by algorithmic procedures, over which they have no control and of which they often have no prior knowledge.

Since the mid-1970s, beginning with shape grammars and computational geometry and continuing through topological properties and morphism, designers and theorists have been concerned with the use of algorithms as a mechanism for exploring formal compositions. These theories have attempted either to automate and enhance existing manual techniques or to explore new uncharted territories of formal behavior. Various methods have been employed in the search for new forms: formal analysis involves the investigation of the properties that describe an architectural subject. Composition, geometrical attributes, and morphological properties obeying Galilean, Newtonian, and, lately, molecular and organic principles are extracted from figural appearances of an object. In contrast, structural analysis deals with the derivation of the motivations and propensities which are implicit within form and which may be used to extract their generative processes. Morphism employs algorithmic processes for the interconnection between seemingly disparate entities and the evolution from one design to another.

Unlike computerization or digitization, the extraction of algorithmic processes is an act of high-level abstraction. It is often equated with rationalism, determinism, or formalism, but more importantly these resources are ultimately in the service of transcendency. Transcendency is the quality of lying beyond the ordinary range of perception. It is the quality of being above and beyond in response to timelessness and spacelessness. Algorithmic structures represent abstract patterns that are not necessarily associated with experience or perception. Furthermore, the observable outputs of algorithms should not be equated with the processes that created them. Marcos Novak makes a distinction between topology and curved surfaces. Topology, he points out, "means simply the study of those relations that remain invariant under transformations and deformations. A notion of continuity is indeed implied in this definition, but the continuity is abstract."[12] Similarly, in *Architectonics of Humanism* Lionel March "seeks an order beyond appearances" as he attempts to "uncover the 'many modes of numbering'" and "looks for the 'warring and opposing elements', which go to make an original microcosm echoing universal harmony."[13] Algorithmic processes result from events that are often neither observable nor predictable and seem to be highly intuitive. These events are made possible by abstraction and ingenuity. For instance, the discovery (or invention) of "hyperspace" resulted from an algorithmic inductive process of projections that map three-dimensional points into four-dimensional ones, yet both the projections and the results are neither predictable nor observable. In this sense, algorithmic processes become a vehicle for exploration that extends beyond the limits of perception.

When comparing contemporary practicing architects such as Thom Mayne, Frank Gehry, and Peter Eisenmann it is necessary to overlook many significant and distinguishing differences in order to identify at least one common theme: the use of the computer as an exploratory formal tool and the increasing dependency of their work on computational methods. The most paradigmatic examples of the last ten years invest in computationally generated partis and diagrams. Through computation, architecture transcends itself beyond the common and predictable. In contrast, computerization provokes Whorfian effects: through the use of commercial applications and the dependency on their design possibilities, the designer's work is at risk of being dictated by the language-tools they use. By unknowingly converting to the constraints of a particular computer application's style, one runs the risk of being associated not with the cutting-edge research, but with a mannerism of "hi-tech" style.

In *Diagram Diaries*,[14] Peter Eisenman's concept of an architectural diagram as an explanatory, analytical, generative, or representational device is directly linked to the principles of human understanding and interpretation. This human-centric approach is implicit within the sphere of subjective phenomena and personal interpretations. Within that realm, any logic that deals with the evaluation or production of form must be, by default, both understandable and open to interpretation. The problem with this approach is that it does not allow thoughts to transcend beyond the sphere of human understanding. In fact, while it praises and celebrates the uniqueness and complexity of the human mind, it also becomes resistant to theories that point out the potential limitations of the human mind. In contrast, algorithmic form is not about perception or interpretation but rather about the process of exploration, codification, and extension of the human mind. Both the algorithmic input and the computer's output are inseparable within a computational system of complementary sources. In this sense, a diagram becomes the embodiment of a process obtainable through a logic of mutual contributions: that of the human mind and that of the machine's extendibility.

Similarly, Euclidean geometry was understood as an extension of human perception. The divinity of its nature can be ultimately linked to its ability to infer abstract concepts that appeal to the mind rather than the eye. Like religion, it was the revelation of an abstract system of relationships that transcended above and beyond the material objects it represented. Similarly, algorithmic form is an extension of human understanding. The mere existence of the term "unimaginable" can be linked to the ability of algorithms to surpass the sphere of human control and prediction. Like meta-structures,[15] algorithmic forms are manifestations of inductive processes that describe, extend and often surpass the designer's intellect.

There is often confusion about ownership of algorithmic forms. Intellectual property is defined as the ownership of ideas and control over the tangible or virtual representation of those ideas. Traditionally, designers maintain full intellectual property rights over their designs or manifestations thereof, based on the assumption that they own and control their ideas. This is not always the case with algorithmic forms. While the hints, clues, or suggestions for an algorithm may be intellectual property of the designer-programmer, the resulting tangible or virtual representations of those ideas is not necessarily under the control of their author. Algorithms employ induction, regression, randomness, recursion, cellular automata, probability, Markov chains, or quantum computation, to name a few, the outcomes of which are unknown, unpredictable, and unimaginable. If there is an intellectual root to these processes it must be sought in a world that extends beyond human understanding.[16] Both the notions of "unknown" and "unimaginable" escape from human understanding since both negate two of the last resorts of human intellect, those of knowledge and imagination. In fact, as Novak points out, while the clause "if-then" is a syllogistic structure that leads on to new knowledge, the clause "if-then-else" involves the alternative "else" that may point to the opposite of knowledge, that is, to "that which does not follow from its roots, or, indeed, that whose roots can no longer be traced, or have become irrelevant, or are unknown, or follow from principles outside previous understanding."[17]

A paradigm shift is defined as a gradual change in the collective way of thinking. It is the change of basic assumptions, values, goals, beliefs, expectations, theories, and knowledge. It is about transformation, transcendence, advancement, evolution, and transition. While paradigm shift is closely related to scientific advancements, its true effect is in the collective realization that a new theory or model requires understanding traditional concepts in new ways, rejects old assumptions, and replaces them with new. For T.S. Kuhn,[18] scientific revolutions occur during those periods when at least two paradigms coexist, one traditional and at least one new. The paradigms are incommensurable, as are the concepts used to understand and explain basic facts and beliefs. The two live in different worlds. The movement from the old to a new paradigm is called a *paradigm shift*.

Traditionally, the dominant paradigm for discussing and producing architecture has been that of human intuition and ingenuity. For the first time perhaps, a paradigm shift is being formulated that outweighs previous ones.[19] Algorithmic design employs methods and devices that have no precedent. If architecture is to embark into the alien world of algorithmic form, its design methods should also incorporate computational processes. If there is a form beyond comprehension it will lie within the algorithmic domain. While human intuition and ingenuity may be the starting point, the computational and combinatorial capabilities of computers must also be integrated.

Notes

1 The work in this area is as old as computer-aided design. An early attempt was MIT's BUILD system, which would take a building program, indicating dimensions and connections for each space. The computer then arranged the spaces, thus solving the problem. This approach has since been used extensively for solving complex design problems that are related to arranging parameters in optimum ways. These approaches focus on the functionality of the design scheme and do not take into account aesthetic or artistic parameters. In areas such as the design of computer chips, nuclear plants, or hospitals, automatic spatial allocation plays a very important role, even today. See Dietz, A., *Dwelling House, Construction* Cambridge: MIT Press, 1974, and Yessios, C., Parent B., Brown, W. and Terzidis, C., "CKAAD Expert: A Computer and Knowledge Aided Architectural Design Expert", in *Design Theory 88*, NSF Grantee Workshop on Design Theory and Methodology, Rensselaer Polytechnic Institute, Troy, NY, 1988, pp. 1–8.

2 Greg Lynn reveals that "because of the stigma and fear of releasing control of the design process to software, few architects have attempted to use the computer as a schematic, organizing and generative medium for design". See Lynn, G., *Animate Form*, New York: Princeton Architectural Press, 1999, p. 19.

3 In response to this discrepancy, the ancient Greeks devised a "fair" method of acknowledgement of authorship. The Pythagorean theorem, the spiral of Archimedes, and Euclidean geometry are

attempts to give proper credit to the authors regardless of the status of their subjects as inventions or discoveries.

4 The term algorithmic is often connected with complexity. While the objective or result of an algorithm may be complex, the strategy itself does not necessarily follow that complexity. For instance, chaos is the study of how simple systems can generate complicated behavior.

5 Perault, the architect of the peristyle of the Louvre, argued that architecture is a fantastic art of pure invention. He asserted that architecture really exists in the mind of the designer and that there is no connection to the natural world. In addition, architecture as an imaginative art obeys its own rules which are internal and personal to each designer, and that is why most creators are vaguely aware of the rules of nature and yet produce excellent pieces of art. A similar point was also argued by Giovanni Battista Vico. In his work *The New Science* (1744), Vico argued that one can know only by imagining. The twisting of language and meaning can lead one to discover new worlds of fantasy. He argued that one can know only what one makes. Only God can understand nature, because it is his creation. Humans, on the other hand, can understand civilization, because they made it. "The world of civil society has certainly been made by men, and its principles are therefore to be found within the modification of our own human mind."

6 In its colloquial sense, computerization refers to the process of furnishing with a computer or a computer system.

7 Julia, G., "Mémoire sur l'itération des fonctions rationnelles", *Journal de Math. Pure et Appl.* vol. 8, 1918, pp. 47–245.

8 Mandelbrot, Benoit B., *The Fractal Geometry of Nature*, New York: W.H. Freeman, 1983.

9 See Cuff, D., "One Educator's Thoughts on Design Software's Profound Effects on Design Thinking and Teaching", *Architectural Record*, vol. 9, 2001, pp. 200–206. In this article, Cuff considers that computing is "one of the most important transformations of the contemporary profession" and that today "computing has become a populist skill".

10 The works of Herbert Simon and Allen Newel in the 1960s and 1970s are undoubtedly some of the best examples of the study of artificial intelligence. Newell, A., *Unified Theories of Cognition*, Cambridge, MA: Harvard University Press, 1990 and Simon, H.A., *The Science of the Artificial*, Cambridge MA: MIT Press, 1981.

11 Lynn, G. in *Animate Form*, op. cit. p. 19, describes machine intelligence "as that of mindless connections."

12 Novak continues:

> A cube is not less topological than a blob. However, when working algorithmically, what remains invariant is the algorithm, so that a new notion of topology, 'variable topology' is introduced. While the variations in the space of the parameters and control structures that implement the algorithm may be continuous, the product of the algorithm may be to show tears and discontinuities and ever fracture into a cloud of particles or an explosion of shards.

See Novak, Marcos, "Transarchitectures and Hypersurfaces", in *Architecture and Science*, ed. G. Di Cristina, London: AD Press, 2001, pp. 153–157.

13 See March, L., *Architectonics of Humanism: Essays on Number in Architecture*, Chichester: Academy Editions, 1998, p. ix.

14 See Eisenman, Peter, *Diagram Diaries*, New York: Universe Publishing, 1999, p. 27.

15 The prefix meta- indicates one level of description higher. If X is some concept, then meta-X is data about, or processes operating on, X. For example, meta-syntax is a syntax for specifying syntax, meta-language is a language used to discuss language, meta-data is data about data, and meta-reasoning is reasoning about reasoning (definition taken from the *Free On-line Dictionary of Computing*).

16 Sir Karl Popper argued that the world as a whole consists of three interconnected worlds. World One is the world of physical objects and their properties – with their energies, forces, and motions; World Two is the subjective world of states of consciousness, or of mental states – with intentions, feelings, thoughts, dreams, memories, and so on, in individual minds. World Three is the world of

objective contents of thought, especially of scientific and poetic thoughts and of works of art. World Three is a human product, a human creation, which creates in turn theoretical systems with their own domains of autonomy. See Popper, Karl R., *The Logic of Scientific Discovery*, New York: Harper & Row, 1968.

17 See Novak, Marcos, "Alien Space: The Shock of the View", Article reproduced from *Art + Technology* Supplement of CIRCA vol. 90, pp. 12–13.

18 See Kuhn, Thomas S., *The Structure of Scientific Revolutions*, 3rd edn, Chicago, IL: University of Chicago Press, 1996.

19 Peter Eisenman referred to the idea of an electronic paradigm shift in architecture in 1992. He wrote:

> During the fifty years since the Second World War, a paradigm shift has taken place that should have profoundly affected architecture: this was the shift from the mechanical paradigm to the electronic one. This change can be simply understood by comparing the impact of the role of the human subject on such primary modes of reproduction as the photograph and the fax; the photograph within the mechanical paradigm, the fax within the electronic one.

Eisenman P., "Visions' Unfolding: Architecture in the Age of Electronic Media", *Domus*, vol. 734, 1992, pp. 17–24.

Epi(dia)logue

The following dialogue is based on excerpts from an on-line chat discussion that appeared on www.archinect.com between 01/08/03 and 01/28/03 (modified):
Persons of the Dialogue

Theoretical Me
Alien
Reverse engineer
Discussion
JS
Name

Theoretical Me 01/08/03–20:51

At risk of revealing myself as an ignoramus, what is computation?

Is this mysterious scripting necessary for rendering? Are you writing your own programs to do functions and model architecture? Are these "plug-ins" for extending programs? Am I totally off?

Alien 01/08/03–23:17

Computation is a term that differs from, but is often confused with, computerization. While computation is the procedure of calculating, i.e., determining something by mathematical or logical methods, computerization is the act of entering, processing, or storing information in a computer or a computer system. Computerization is about automation, mechanization, digitization, and conversion. Generally, it involves the digitization of entities or processes that are preconceived, predetermined, and well defined. In contrast, computation is about the exploration of indeterminate, vague, unclear, and often ill-defined processes; because of its exploratory nature, computation aims at emulating or extending the human intellect.

The dominant mode of utilizing computers in architecture today is that of computerization; entities or processes that are already conceptualized in the designer's mind are entered, manipulated, or stored on a computer system. In contrast, computation or computing, as a computer-based design tool, is generally limited. The problem with this situation is that designers do not take advantage of the computational power of the computer. Instead some venture into manipulations or criticisms of computer models as if they were products of computation.

Presently, an alternative choice is being formulated that may escape these dialectically opposed strategies: algorithmic design. It involves the designation of software programs to generate space and form from the rule-based logic inherent in architectural programs, typologies, building code, and language itself. Instead of direct programming, the codification of design intention using scripting languages available in three-dimensional packages can build consistency, structure, coherency, traceability, and intelligence into computerized three-dimensional form. By using scripting languages designers can go beyond the mouse, transcending the factory-set limitations of current three-dimensional software. Algorithmic design does not eradicate differences but incorporates both computational complexity and creative use of computers. For architects, algorithmic design enables the role of the designer to shift from architecture programming to programming architecture. Rather than investing in arrested conflicts, computational terms might be better exploited by this alternative choice. For the first time perhaps, architectural design might be aligned with neither formalism nor rationalism but with intelligent form and traceable creativity.

Discussion. 01/09/03–02:52

I wonder whether logic can resolve everything in architecture. This sounds like a neo-modernist project: an attempt to resolve everything through scientific logic. However, allow me to have my doubts. I remember that during a lecture on algorithmic architecture, one of the students asked the lecturer whether there is any programmatic necessity which violates the mathematical structure and the lecturer refused to answer that question.

Technically, many teachers in schools of architecture make claims about the power of scripting languages. However, the sole purpose of these languages is mere representation. Modeling is an imitation of reality and scripting is for addressing representation only. Therefore, teachers and students should understand the limitations of scripting and open up a discussion about the difference between imitation and representation.

Algorithmic architecture is inspiring but risky. It is more of an ideology, a utopia, or a myth, which may open up more discussions. I really appreciate that someone started this thread because this is a very important issue now not only in architecture but even in our everyday life.

Reverse engineer 01/09/03–03:42

I read this in a paper by Moravec and want to contribute it to the discussion. I quote:

> The most powerful experimental supercomputers in 1998, composed of thousands or tens of thousands of the fastest microprocessors and costing tens of millions of dollars, can do a few million MIPS (i.e. million instructions per second). They are within striking distance of being powerful enough to match human brainpower, but are unlikely to be applied to that end. Why tie up a rare twenty-million-dollar asset to develop one ersatz-human, when millions of inexpensive original-model humans are available? Such machines are needed for high-value scientific calculations, mostly physical simulations, having no cheaper substitutes.[1]

Alien 01/09/03–06:51

I think that there are still some misconceptions about the role of the computer in the process of design. Design, like many other mental processes, at the information-processing level has nothing specifically neural about it. The functional equivalence between brains and computers does not imply any structural equivalence at an anatomical level (e.g., equivalence of neurons with circuits). Theories of information processes are not equivalent to theories of neural or electronic mechanisms for information processing. Even though, physically, computers may appear to be a set of mindless connections, at the information level they are the materialization of mathematical and syllogistic procedures.

The word "tool" is often used to describe the synergistic interaction of designers with computers. A tool is defined as an instrument used in the performance of an operation. The connotative notion of a tool implies control, power, dominance, skill, and artistry. A pen, for instance, is a device that allows one to perform or facilitate the manual or mechanical work of writing or drawing. The capabilities, potency, and limitations of a tool are known or estimated in advanced. This is not the case with computers performing inductive algorithmic computations. Neither is their capacity or potency understood, nor can their limitations be pre-estimated. Indeed, designers are frequently amazed by processes performed by algorithmic procedures, over which they have no control and of which they often have no prior knowledge.

JS 01/09/03–18:26

I still doubt the efficiency of algorithmic design. My experience is that the amount of effort it takes to write and test e.g. genetic algorithms could have been used to design the building itself. It is as if the algorithm itself is a kind of an arbitrary design, or more specifically, a kind of vague representation. Anyone having tried to make evaluations of procedures for phenotypes must have come across this problem, found even in very simple systems. The "scientific logic" is tied more to the method than the outcome. Still, I don't really believe that computer-based design can finally free architects from all restrictions in representations or, as you say, tools. I agree with Robin Evans saying that we can only find freedom in the rigor of techniques, being fully aware of their limitations.[2]

Reverse engineer 01/10/03–00:13

I doubt we have exhausted the potency of a pen, anyway, even though we live in an era of finding ways to deconstruct or reinvent a pen. I totally agree with JS in the exploration of genetic processes – using algorithm as the fundamental building blocks of things. Yeah Alien . . . Correct me if I understood it wrong. But I still have a problem with it – the machine. According to cognitive science, a computer can do things we humans find difficult, such as count 1 to 1,000. However, computational processing seems to have great difficulties doing things we found very easy, such as picking a pair of socks from a J. Crew catalog. Given the promises of a universal Turing machine, eventually the machine will have the capacity to handle increasingly most difficult tasks, such as picking the socks, but what if it picks the wrong color? What does "the wrong color" mean? What I mean is how can algorithmic processes help us make sense of the world?

Alien 01/10/03–00:50

Most algorithms are tailored to automate tedious manual methods; yet, there is a certain category of algorithms that are not aimed at predictable results. Their inductive strategy is to explore generative processes or to simulate complex phenomena. Such inductive algorithms can be regarded as extensions to human thinking and therefore may allow one to leap into areas of unpredictable, unimaginable, and often inconceivable potential. For instance, artificial neural networks are systems of algorithms that simulate the human brain's functions. They are being used in classification, forecasting, and modeling applications. In making determinations, neural networks use several principles, including gradient-based training, fuzzy logic, genetic algorithms, and Bayesian methods. What distinguishes these algorithmic processes from common algorithms is that their behavior is often non-predictable and that frequently they produce patterns of thought and results that amaze even their own creators. Similarly in design, shape grammars, mathematical models, topological properties, genetic systems, mappings, and morphisms are algorithmic processes aimed at exploring uncommon, unpredictable, and uncharted formal properties and behaviors.

Discussion 01/10/03–02:58

I agree with you about the potential and power of the computer algorithm. However, why do we need something unpredictable, something new? What is the moral value of something "new"? Is it a common goal of everyone to have something new?

Someone would think that we don't have to learn any foreign language since sound recognition and fuzzy logic can help one to translate language from one into another. Computer language would be a global language. However, how can one translate implications, jokes, and cultural specificity through fuzzy logic? How can computer language translate slang which changes from time to time? Scientific logic gives us some hints but not the complete story.

How can we include the cultural otherness, "non-advanced" culture in the development of algorithmic architecture? You know only countries with advanced technology can develop more advanced technology? What can the "new" architecture do to the rest of the world? In reality, the advanced countries develop the avant-garde to maintain their power as being advanced.

This is a myth of modernism and it's persisting. While we underwent the criticism of Modernist architecture in the last fifty years, how can we learn from that criticism?

Alien 01/10/03–04:35

It is not about the notion of new. It is about the notion of different. If it makes you feel better, human's assumed dominance over the machine is only a necessary condition to explain phenomena and build up interpretations. Within the human realm, any logic that deals with the evaluation or production of form must be, by default, both understandable and open to interpretation. The problem with this approach is that it does not allow thoughts to transcend beyond the sphere of human understanding. In fact, while it praises and celebrates the uniqueness and complexity of the human mind, it also becomes resistant to theories that point out the potential limitations of the human mind.

Algorithms employ induction, regression, randomness, recursion, cellular automata, probability, Markov chains, or quantum computation, to name a few, the outcomes of which are unknown, unpredictable, and unimaginable. If there is an intellectual root to these processes it must be sought in a world that extends beyond human understanding. Both the notions of unknown and unimaginable escape from human understanding since both negate two of the last resorts of human intellect, those of knowledge and imagination. In fact, as Novak points out, while the clause "if-then" is a syllogistic structure that leads on to new knowledge, the clause "if-then-else" involves the alternative "else" that may point to the opposite of knowledge, that is, to "that which does not follow from its roots, or, indeed, that whose roots can no longer be traced, or have become irrelevant, or are unknown, or follow from principles outside previous understanding."

Discussion 01/10/03–23:05

To some point I agree with you. Especially when you say, "In fact, while it praises and celebrates the uniqueness and complexity of the human mind, it becomes also resistant to theories that point out the potential limitations of the human mind." It's a very interesting point.

However, I don't agree with this thread of theoretical approach started from Colin Rowe, Peter Eisenman and Greg Lynn. I'm still thinking what an alien form can do. I am afraid that whatever it does, it may get quickly customized by language. For example, when Frank Gehry's "thing" first appeared everyone asked what is this? This challenged, of course, the traditional form of architecture, but now, several years after Bilbao, every city wants to get one Frank Gehry. Instead of challenging the societal concept, it anchors the societal concept.

People already acknowledged that architecture might be like that: a trend. Instead of challenging the societal concept, it anchors a new societal concept.

Alien 01/11/03–00:30

I think you are taking things in the wrong direction. While certain trends or fashions may have influenced or dominated architecture, there are also universal and eternal concepts built into the discipline. Think of geometry. Euclidean geometry was understood as an extension of human perception. The divinity of its nature can be ultimately linked to its ability to infer abstract concepts that appeal to the mind rather than the eye. Like religion, it was the revelation of an abstract system of relationships that transcended above and beyond the material objects it represented. Similarly, algorithmic form is an extension of human understanding. The mere existence of the term "unimaginable" can be linked to the ability of algorithms to surpass the sphere of human control and prediction. Like meta-structures, algorithmic forms are manifestations of inductive processes that describe, extend and often surpass the designer's intellect.

Discussion 01/11/03–02:40

Thanks a lot for your elaboration. It's a very positive discussion around here to me.

I would like to quote a specific real-life example to explain the contradiction of algorithmic architecture . . . In studio, students were asked to use scripting in order to generate some unimaginable alien form. At the second half of the semester, they were asked to make the alien form into architecture, that is, fit a program and a structure in it . . . However, everybody struggled tremendously almost without hope, because the students didn't know how to use logic to "put stuff" in the form. I would say that practical issues, economic, cultural and structural, were fighting one another and no scientific logic could resolve the conflict. In contrast, architects are doing it every day by custom and convention.

I feel sorry that while I criticize algorithmic architecture I do not provide a solution. It is not helpful at all but I'm searching for it.

Alien 01/11/03–03:03

A paradigm shift is defined as a gradual change in the collective way of thinking. It is the change of basic assumptions, values, goals, beliefs, expectations, theories, and knowledge. It is about transformation, transcendence, advancement, evolution, and transition. While paradigm shift is closely related to scientific advancements, its true effect is in the collective realization that a new theory or model requires understanding traditional concepts in new ways, rejects old assumptions, and replaces them with new. For T.S. Kuhn, scientific revolutions occur during those periods when at least two paradigms coexist, one traditional and at least one new. The paradigms are incommensurable, as are the concepts used to understand and explain basic facts and beliefs. The two live in different worlds. The movement from the old to a new paradigm is called a paradigm shift.

Traditionally, the dominant paradigm for discussing and producing architecture has been that of human intuition and ingenuity. For the first time perhaps, a paradigm shift is being formulated that outweighs previous ones. Algorithmic design employs methods and devices that have no precedent. If architecture is to embark into the alien world of algorithmic form, its design methods should also incorporate computational processes. If there is a form beyond comprehension it will lie within the algorithmic domain. While human intuition and ingenuity may be the starting point, the computational and combinatorial capabilities of computers must also be integrated.

Name 01/11/03–04:28

Right. And the same could be said of algorithmic design in every field this way. What are the specific issues endemic to architectural design? Your statements are actually quite vague (maybe not as much as mine) and don't really define the concerns of algorithmic design within this field. What you are saying is the same crux for all fields exploring algorithms.

Discussion 01/17/03–23:28

But how can one know one is inside the paradigm shift while one is undergoing shifting? Some say that we're undergoing paradigm shift because the biotechnology advancement starts to question the human nature.

I always think that the shift does not come until certain people have prophesized something to come. The paradigm shift doesn't exist until someone says so.

It sounds like a Modernist project: while it advocates changing the world and bringing things to another stage, the world is changing already anyway.

It seems like the unknown horizon is much larger than any map we could chart. Then, how will we be able to position ourselves within this unprecedented space/plane? Maybe mapping no long applies on this alien terrain. What then?

Alien 01/23/03–05:38

Computational formal explorations do not eradicate human imagination but rather extend its potential limitations. Computation is not a substitute for human creativity and therefore cannot be antagonistic. Rather it provides the means for exploration, experimentation, and investment in an alternative realm. For the first time perhaps, form might be aligned with neither arbitrary creativity nor computational determinism but with creative computation and computational creativity.

Conversely, human intuition is characterized by originality, expressiveness, and imagination. While in the human world intuition has been an underlying assumption for many design activities, in the world of computation a more rational, confined, organized, and methodical model exists. It suggests efficiency, effectiveness, and productivity, while, at the same time, it may be resistant to emotion, humor, irony, metaphor, or analogy.

Name 01/27/03–18:03

Algorithms are tools to play with possibilities, they are ways of speeding up processes we cannot do on our own at such a rate, and, as stated, allow us to program spaces wherein new forms of logistical relations can rear their own heads. But the endpoint of algorithms is not simply to generate through randomness, but the contrary: it is also to tailor logic in order to respond to all possible stimuli in a way that we cannot possibly predict on our own. Algorithms represent logic, and then in turn, those generated representations can set out to form new logical connections for us, so we can obtain a symbiotic language for observing, controlling, experimenting, and rewriting logic. We make the parameters by which to conduct research, and write intelligence into the game. Yes, the search that this will evolve computation beyond something initially comprehensible is exciting, that it will one day expose some logic perhaps that we thought was infinitely incomprehensible is all about the search for logical integrity, pushing into the blackness of the logical process itself.

Algorithms are the dreams for new patterns in logic. They also show us as many fallacies in our logic as they have potential to reveal any new evolutionary functionality. Constantly send out new fluctuating patterns of systems into what we want to test as a void, and see if anything comes back. This approach itself gets at the root of logical inquiry, challenging the integrity of what is referred to as predictability, and in the end may turn up brand new forms through a birth rite of mutation and computation. However, I think we also end up unknowingly relying on algorithms that cannot always possibly be tested or understood enough. And we find ourselves depending on an unreliable artificial intelligence, of which we have no idea why it is not functioning properly. In terms of design and architecture, I simply feel that right now algorithmic design is merely a trend, something new to explore, it managed to churn out some new forms, and bang! we have mass marketing of algorithmic newness bending around the planet.

JS 01/27/03–18:20

I believe it is true that "algorithmic methods" present us with a range of optional designs. It can be argued that this is equally true for ordinary (non-computer) methods; trial and error is a part of every creative act. Generally, genetic algorithms (which are a kind of basic algorithmic design method) work with combinations of random numbers and genotypes. The genotypes are translated into a geometrical form, a phenotype. This phenotype is then evaluated by a mathematical procedure (which might test stability, shadows, topological depth etc.) and something often called "the eyeball-test" which includes the preferences of the designer. The phenotypes with the highest values are then "bred" with each other to create new (and hopefully more efficient) genotypes which are then grown and evaluated again etc.

Now, this seems like a very logical technique, but a programmer/designer soon discovers that there are some very difficult steps in the process. First, the procedure translating the genotypes into phenotypes is already a very design-like step, since we in fact have to limit the geometrical possibilities. Second, the procedure of evaluating the phenotypes poses difficult questions for the architect: should structural stability account for 30 per cent or 35 per cent of the phenotypes' value? Such small changes can affect the solution significantly. Third, the breeding procedure might become very inefficient, creating e.g. super-stable but "ugly" phenotypes.

Anyway, as you might notice, I'm fascinated by algorithmic design, but I've also studied it sufficiently to be aware of its limitations. I'm also a skeptic about statements like "challenging traditional values", since it is often unclear what this really means. Many architects might use it as an argument to design and build geometrically complex surfaces, as if the right angle would be the biggest threat to freedom in architecture. I'm afraid we're going from one rigid system to an even more rigid one.

Discussion 01/28/03–16:11

The issue of appearance is problematic, however not unique to consciously algorithmically derived objects. While CAD programs represent the inherent algorithm behind each object, algorithmic design is taking advantage of the mathematics and consciously manipulating it directly.

The nature of algorithmic design is to try to create mathematical "environments" consisting of rules, absolutes, variables, and even random values that are possibly derived from the design problem at hand. Then, within these environments, allow the computational power of the machine to "grow" appropriate forms, and in the end use the computer beyond simply a container for "hand" (mouse) drawn answers.

The biggest issue at hand is whether the input of the designer is too far removed from the production of an answer so that it misses some humanistic appeal. Or if using humanistic-derived variables and values to guide the algorithmic creation in the end creates an inappropriate solution due to misfit.

I believe the fact is that it is inevitable that this process will develop. I don't think this means that all structures will look alike. But the concept of defining the spatial requirements, and then using our existing knowledge of structures, energy efficiency, lighting, egress, building codes, cultural values, material capabilities, even cost as plugging algorithmic values or ranges of values and then tying them into CAD programs, can generate digital shop drawings that are sent to rapid prototyping printers. Form and design can be controlled through user-defined geometries, spatial complexities, considered variables, or even custom-made algorithmic plug-ins that are completely user defined and user set that address any possible value. The point is, however, that this opens the door to the type of geometries that many architects have dreamt of: geometry of great complexity and multiplicity. While it may streamline the process behind typical forms, it also opens the door to forms of complexity that we have yet to realize.

Acknowledgment

This is to thank all the people involved in this dialogue for their insights and great ideas. While the purpose of this dialogue was to seek a diversity of opinions, some of the contributing peoples' original comments may have been altered.

Notes

1 Moravec H., "When will computer hardware match the human brain?", *Journal of Evolution and Technology*, vol. 1, 1998 pp. 1–2.

2 One of Robin Evans' points was that pictures do not provide all that architects need, suggesting that there is much more within the scope of the architect's vision of a project than what can be drawn. Within that logic, tools and techniques, such as those of projective geometry, can only lead to fully expressive schemes when their limitations are understood, comprehended, and dealt with. See Evans, R., *The Projective Cast: Architecture and Its Three Geometries*, Cambridge, MA: MIT Press, 1995.

Index

www.study-guides.com
www.study-guides.com
www.study-guides.com
www.study-guides.com

www.ingramcontent.com/pod-product-compliance
Lightning Source LLC
LaVergne TN
LVHW082343011026
849160LV00025B/1593